The Mountains Know ARIZONA

Book Designer: MARY WINKELMAN VELGOS
Photography Editor: PETER ENSENBERGER
Copy Editors: PK PERKIN McMAHON, EVELYN HOWELL
Book Editor: BOB ALBANO
Map and Illustrations: KEVIN KIBSEY

Library of Congress Control Number 2002111894
ISBN 1-893860-87-6

First printing, 2003. Printed in Hong Kong.

Published by the Book Division of *Arizona Highways*
magazine, a monthly publication of the Arizona
Department of Transportation, 2039 West Lewis Avenue,
Phoenix, Arizona 85009.
Telephone: (602) 712-2200
Web site: www.arizonahighways.com

Publisher: WIN HOLDEN
Managing Editor: BOB ALBANO
Associate Editor: EVELYN HOWELL
Associate Editor: PK PERKIN McMAHON
Art Director: MARY WINKELMAN VELGOS
Director of Photography: PETER ENSENBERGER
Production Director: CINDY MACKEY
Production Coordinator: KIM ENSENBERGER

Images of the Land and
Stories of Its People

The Mountains Know
ARIZONA

TEXT BY ROSE HOUK   PHOTOGRAPHS BY MICHAEL COLLIER

To Bill and Dot Collier,
who led the way to Arizona

Many people gave freely of their time and resources for our research. We thank Helen Fairley, Pat Stein, and Dennis Lund for providing documents, maps, and personal knowledge. Nick Berezenko reminisced about his amazing Little Colorado River adventure. Tom Robinson took us on an impromptu tour of Casa Malpais by Springerville. Sister Welch gave freely of her time at the Jacob Hamblin home in Santa Clara, Utah, and sent us on our way with juicy peaches. Rose Minetti of Arizona State University Library dug into the archives. Bill Adams kept us afloat, while Tom Carpenter, Bob Hall, Bob Webb, and Ivo Lucchitta shared insights about Arizona's landscapes. Vinson Etcitty showed us Turquoise Hill. Tom and Edith Beatty and Smokey and Judy Knowlton gave unreserved hospitality. And friends Ed Peacock and Bill Burke were the best of camping companions. Finally, deep thanks to Bob Albano, PK McMahon, Evelyn Howell, Mary Velgos, Pete Ensenberger, Cindy Mackey, Kim Ensenberger, and every one of the tireless, enthusiastic staff at *Arizona Highways*.

Perhaps I can tell you something of what I have seen in these 2 years of wandering; but I shall never be able to tell you the grandeur of these mountains, nor the glory of color that wraps the burning sands at their feet. We shoot arrows at the sun in vain; yet still we shoot.

John C. Van Dyke

I am from the flat lands, and so mountains forever will be mystical to me. And I, like author John C. Van Dyke, spent 2 years wandering amid some of Arizona's incredible mountain ranges. Mountains ring the edges and rise in the interior, some like mirages floating in low desert valleys, others like adornments added to high, forested plateaus. They gather clouds and beget rivers that flow out into cactus country, cow country, timber country, and copper country.

Originally, photographer Michael Collier and I had an idea to do a book on the state's mountains. But *Arizona Highways* Books editor Bob Albano took that idea and turned it at an angle. Use the mountains as platforms, he advised, and from them talk about what you see and think about. This would not be a book about "bagging" peaks, but one that tells the history of the land and the people of this amazing state from the vantage of its high places. Thus was born *The Mountains Know Arizona*.

We sat down with a map and chose 10 ranges. Starting at the top and going clockwise around the state, we selected Navajo Mountain, the Chuska/Lukachukai range, San Francisco Peaks, White Mountains, Four Peaks, Huachucas, Santa Catalinas, Kofas, Hualapais, and Uinkarets with Mount Trumbull.

Some were old friends; some we barely knew. Of course we could have spent years looking from atop many other mountains — the Pinalenos are so high, the Chiricahuas are so broad. But 10 seemed like a nice, round number. We aimed for a good geographic representation and for the stories the mountains would let us tell.

From Flagstaff, we traveled to all 10, covering more than 30,000 miles and gazing upon uncounted numbers of sunrises and sunsets, the kind that only Arizona can produce. Serendipity led us much of the way. We followed the footsteps of pathfinder and peacemaker Jacob Hamblin, who escorted Maj. John Wesley Powell to a meeting with Shivwits Indians at the foot of Mount Trumbull on the Arizona Strip. We helped make fry bread for a hundred Navajo

A beguiling sunset gets extra play over the waters of Crescent Lake in the White Mountains, preceding pages. Aspen and conifer forests grace the mountains east of Alpine, left.

11

Tasting somewhat like spinach, miner's lettuce, above, is a delicacy found in damp, shaded spots in Aravaipa Canyon.

gathered in Tsaile on the west side of the Chuskas. We talked to crusty ranchers in the White Mountains, where we also watched for bears and listened for wolves. We savored the primal call of sandhill cranes rising off the Willcox Playa on a frigid winter morning. We luxuriated in fields of desert wildflowers, poked around old mines, walked countless canyons, and boated stretches of the Colorado River. We were blessed too by the renewal of past acquaintances and the generosity of complete strangers who took interest in what we were doing and gave of their time, expertise, and specific knowledge of place.

I was worried, at first, that we ran the risk of repetition — that we would be seeing one pine forest after another, and that would be all. I should have known better; there can be no more fascinating diversity anywhere on earth than in the mountains of Arizona. Each is unique, with a distinct profile, a particular geology, and special life forms. Tundra on the summit of the San

Francisco Peaks above my home in Flagstaff, glorious rolling grasslands and flowing rivers in the White Mountains, fecund Madrean woodlands of the Huachucas, sere face of the Kofas in the driest quarter of the state.

My first sight of the San Francisco Peaks some 30 years ago aroused my imagination. I had never seen anything like their graceful sweep piercing a blue sky. They exuded the power of mountains, how they draw you in, how they define a particular geography and perspective of a place, why they are regarded as the sacred homes of the gods.

The work on this book involved a personal journey, too. The mountains provided solace after the death of my father, who also loved mountains, and they were Michael's and my destination after one of our nation's great tragedies. A week after September 11, 2001, we anchored a houseboat in Lake Powell at the foot of Navajo Mountain. We heard no news and were unaware of what was transpiring in the world. The second night, a storm moved in slowly from the west. When it finally reached us, it slashed out with knives of lightning, eerily flashing on the sandstone walls, continuing its fury for more than an hour. All I could think was that War God, who lives on Navajo Mountain, was sending a dire warning.

With each trip out, I came to appreciate what it means to be a photographer, chasing every shard of light. How you can go out and simply look, and see, new country. And how much of my own history I've gathered in Arizona, now my heart's home.

Rose Houk

Flagstaff, Arizona

Easter weekend 2002

A potpourri of miners' debris from the Kofa Mountains' Polaris Mine seems to be weathering back into nature, below.

My family climbed Squaw Peak in 1959, soon after we moved to Phoenix. I was so excited to see our new home down there near Bethany Home Road that — with a young boy's bad judgment — I threw a rock as hard and as far as I could. It traveled about 4 feet before clobbering my dad squarely in the back. He yelped, and I stared down at my pigeon-toed feet. So began my love affair with Arizona from its mountains.

Ah, Arizona. We would pile into the '55 Ford and head toward Sheep's Crossing, Big Lake, and the White Mountains, babbling all the way about fat, pink trout. There were magical times beneath the Mogollon Rim when my sister and I would explore the chaparral country around Payson. In high school, I would career from town on Friday nights in a friend's jeep, spending weekends in a line shack high in the Sierra Ancha range. Then came college at Northern Arizona University's mountain campus in Flagstaff, where I majored in "Gee-Whiz Geology." Mountains have always been mileposts marking my life in Arizona.

It's been a great honor and opportunity to be invited by *Arizona Highways* to revisit places I first saw 40 or more years ago. I suppose it would have been cheating to photograph all of this from an airplane. Bob Albano, our editor who was well aware of my aerial proclivities, put his foot down from the start. "No more than one picture out of 10 taken from that noisy airplane of yours!"

Yessir, boss. So I strapped on my camera pack — and Rose packed her pencils — and we headed out to rediscover our home.

Photography is a jealous lover; she requires unswerving concentration. I take a few steps, stop, and listen. I form my fingers into a rectangle against the skyline, imagining the perspective a 135mm lens would yield, then a 75mm, before deciding on a 210mm Schneider. As photographer Dick Arentz said, one walks in progressively tighter circles until zeroing in on just the right angle, just the right light.

Photography, more than any other endeavor I can imagine, connects me body and soul to a landscape. In my 35-pound pack, beyond the ArcaSwiss camera and its five lenses, I carry a stopwatch, lens paper, compass, snake-bite kit, and a liter of water. In my mind, I gratefully carry the history of those who have been out here before me — Jack Dykinga, Larry Ulrich, George Huey. Is there anything new under the sun? Yes and no. They've been here before, shivering, waiting for this same early-morning light.

The rugged Vermilion Cliffs, left, provide habitat for desert bighorn sheep and California condors.

15

Bigtooth maples, below, inject fiery color into the confines of Fry Canyon, south of Flagstaff.

Serpentine walls of Navajo sandstone define Oak Canyon, in Utah, following pages.

But having paid homage to those other photographers, I'm surprised again and again by how fresh the world looks when I'm here on my own, peering at a dew-dropped lupine, squinting through a juniper at sunset. I wanted to go beyond Arizona's icons. Monument Valley and Grand Canyon are certainly inspiring, but for this project I also wanted to seek out the state's lesser known pockets. I needed to meet these mountains on their own terms — aspens on Escudilla in October, poppies around Stewart Mountain in March, snow blowing over the San Francisco Peaks in January. The camera forced me to slow down and really look at the details of the landscape in front of me.

Had we not done this book, Rose and I wouldn't have met Budlow Joy down on the Blue in eastern Arizona. His apple trees were breaking with fruit when we visited in September and asked if we could pick a few. With a gesture at once tired and grandiose, he said, "Take 'em; take 'em all." Since his wife had died in the spring, no one made pies at his home anymore. The horses would eat the ones already on the ground.

16

Had we not gone out, we wouldn't have seen that tawny beautiful bobcat on the Colorado River's Topock shore. He moved regally, wasting no motion, watching us float by without changing his pace or course. For a moment, I felt like Santiago, Hemingway's *Old Man*, dreaming no longer of women or wealth, but of lions playing on the beaches of Africa.

Photographing *The Mountains Know Arizona* has felt a lot like coming home. As we drove the 14 miles into Horseshoe Bend on the Salt River, I jabbered endlessly to Rose about our wonderful wilderness river trips of the 1970s, '80s, and '90s. On the way to Mount Trumbull, we followed the same dirt road down which I had herded cattle 20 years earlier. In Sabino Canyon, we relived those exquisite Sunday afternoons, reading by the creek in the shade of a sycamore tree. To be sure, Arizona has changed in the intervening decades. Phoenix has grown wildly, its suburbs metastasizing into the surrounding desert. Mountain bicyclists now bump and grind their way around the foot of the San Francisco Peaks. South of Kingman, hypothetical roads are gridded for miles along the western base of the Hualapai Mountains; incongruous metal street signs vibrate in the wind, waiting for the homes that are sure to follow.

We also found havens along the way — shallow shining ponds, ringed by irises, gracing the roof of the Lukachukais; the trickle of Miller Creek as it teases fallen maple leaves within the Huachucas. I sit now on the edge of Grand Wash Cliffs, north of the Colorado, a hundred miles beyond the nearest pavement. The handful of ranch houses in Hurricane Valley are days away by horseback. From this aerie near Mount Trumbull, I can see into Utah in one direction, into Nevada in another. I can see all the way back into the 19th century in yet a third direction.

In this country, the thin rising wedge of dust behind a pickup 10 miles distant would be cause for interest but not concern. Today I see no one. I eat peaches and sip tea, waiting for the sun to skid into the western horizon. The wind is fresh and the sky is achingly blue. Photographing Arizona from its mountains has been a wonderful way to spend these 2 years, getting to know my home again from the ground up. To walk with my camera has been to witness the beauty that still shines in this world.

Michael Collier
Pigeon Canyon
February 2002

Four Peaks

Four Peaks

Standing Watch Over Phoenix

A Colorado cowboy pointed out to us Arizonans that Four Peaks are pictured on our state's vehicle license plates. Given that we had just come down from the heights of those mountains, it was a little embarrassing that we had failed to notice their purple profile emblazoned on aluminum on our bumper.

The cowboy had pulled over next to us in his big, white pickup truck at the Salt River bridge on New Year's morning. In the bed of his truck lay a bale of hay, an old saddle he had just bought, and some kind of antique scythe. He waved that mean-looking tool a bit menacingly, but he was harmless. He stuck out his hand, introduced himself ("Howdy, Johnny Green's my name."), and groused that he'd been hanging around the town of Roosevelt waiting for his buddies to arrive to rope some cattle. But they hadn't shown up yet. Whiskey supplies were running low, and he was getting bored. Maybe that was the reason he stopped to talk with us.

Seeing Michael's camera, he wanted to know if we had any pictures with us, "old pictures," he said. We allowed that we didn't have any, then explained that we were working on a book involving Arizona mountains. It was then that

The rugged topography of the Four Peaks region east of Phoenix supports an astonishing array of plant life, from pines to poppies. Adjacent to Red Creek above the Verde River, preceding pages, Mexican poppies thrive. At left, Parker Creek nourishes a riparian ribbon in the Sierra Ancha.

he called our attention to the artwork on our license plate. I said I was interested in old pictures too, especially ones showing construction of Roosevelt Dam in the early 1900s. Darn if he didn't know of some, on the wall of a cafe down the road.

After we talked a little longer (while he waved at every other cowboy-inhabited truck that rumbled across the skinny bridge), we said our farewells. At the recommended cafe we stopped in for a bite to eat and a look at those photos. Our new acquaintance had steered us right, for the walls were decked out with wonderful black-and-white enlargements of the men who hauled the freight and cut the stone to build Roosevelt Dam, the first dam on the Salt River and one of the first in the federal government's fledgling program to "reclaim" the nation's dry lands in the first decade of the 20th century.

At the foot of Four Peaks begins a string of four reservoirs. The mnemonic S-C-A-R spells their sequence as they stair-step up the Salt River — Saguaro, Canyon, Apache, and finally the silver waters of Roosevelt Lake, the first and largest. The lakes were formed by dams that have stanched the river's flow for the time being and enclosed the words Salt River in parentheses on the forest map.

Four Peaks, incisors of old quartzite gnawing at the sky, draw a dramatic conclusion to the south end of the mighty Mazatzal Mountains. With the Mazatzals to the north, and the Superstition Mountains pinching in on the south, the Salt River threads through the "eye" of a geologic needle on its way west into the Sonoran Desert.

This quartet of peaks, and the quartet of lakes now encircling their base, have profoundly shaped Arizona's cultural landscape. For well nigh a century, these lakes have provided the water for fields of cotton, groves of oranges, and hedges of oleanders, not to mention the millions of people living in the state's largest — and ever-expanding — metropolitan area. Writes essayist Bruce Berger, "The history of Phoenix, from outpost through oasis to elephantiasis, is written in channeled water."

To begin appreciating the importance of water in this desert, we go back at least to the Hohokam people. For more than a thousand years, digging with nothing more than wood sticks, these master irrigators excavated hundreds of miles of canals into the recalcitrant caliche soil of the Phoenix Basin.

While the word desert implies barren, the Sonoran Desert is anything but that. Wildflowers such as lupine, below, explode on the desert with just a little rain.

Farther upstream on the Salt, the Salado people flourished for a few hundred years doing much the same. Their cliffside aerie, preserved at Tonto National Monument just northwest of Globe, looks out spectacularly on what was then the Salt River — now Roosevelt Lake. Into the mid-19th century, the Pima Indians drew irrigation water from the Salt as well, succeeding quite well at farming.

Enter Jack Swilling, a fiery Confederate veteran who had come to Phoenix and freighted wild hay for John Y.T. Smith to the Army's Fort McDowell. Curious about those ancient Hohokam canals, Swilling sniffed a better opportunity — dig a canal to distribute the waters of the Salt River to fields in the valley. With modest funds and a handful of men, in 1867 he revamped one of those old canals. The Swilling Ditch (located within earshot of what is now Sky Harbor Airport) was the Salt River Valley's first modern irrigation canal. Water was turned out onto fields of alfalfa, barley, and wheat, and other canals soon followed. Companies formed around the canals, first run as cooperative enterprises but soon as profit-making corporations.

At the beginning, Jack Swilling's bet was on the money. The sparkling promise of water drew thousands of farmers to the Salt River Valley. In 1870, a couple of years after the ditch was completed, 235 people called the valley home. Twenty years later, there were 11,000 souls. Boosterism took the form of handsome, hand-tinted booklets such as one published by *Sunset* magazine's Homeseekers' Bureau. The author ballyhooed the valley as the Land of Milk and Honey, "where 1 acre yields 40 bushels of wheat or 10 tons of alfalfa … where strawberries ripen every month of the year … where soil and climate work together for health and prosperity." The valley is a "fertile oasis … ready for the plow," and "the man who does not believe in the advantages of moisture at the right time, and in the cash value of a winterless climate, had better not come here."

The author, however, did not dwell on the fact that the valley receives a mere 6 inches of precipitation in an average year, and sometimes half of that courtesy of a single summer storm.

Had the new farmers been able to compare notes with their Hohokam predecessors, they'd have gained some information about the Salt River's unruly propensities. Only a year after Swilling's ditch was finished, the river rampaged into a flood, tearing out brush and rock weirs as if it were child's

And, at left, a diverse collection of mesquite trees, saguaro cactus, and cottonwood trees grows in close association in this rich desert.

After a day of intense heat and harsh light, the desert begins to come to life just before sunset. Animals stir and the light softens. Below, cholla, prickly pear, paloverde, and saguaro form a garden above Apache Lake.

A pair of elderly saguaros, right, stands in front of cottonwoods on Armer Creek above Lake Roosevelt. Other saguaros, following pages, stand out among plants lining the Verde River, a major tributary of the Salt River. The Verde flows west of the Mazatzal Mountains and Four Peaks. With its headwaters in the Chino Valley north of Prescott, the Verde runs freely through central Arizona, a vein of life in the desert.

play. More damaging floods came through in 1874 and again in 1890 and 1891. In the next few years, a long drought dried up much of the gamblers' winnings. In the valley, people stood guard with shotguns to ward off anyone who might try to pilfer their water shares. The first flush of prosperity started to pale. Crops shriveled and cultivated acreage dropped more than a fourth by the early years of the new century.

Valley farmers saw one answer: a dam across the river, creating a reservoir to store water and tide them over during dry times. The chosen site was at a narrow spot where Tonto Creek flowed south to mingle with the Salt River. The federal government would pay for this Tonto Dam (soon renamed Theodore Roosevelt Dam), while the landowners buying the water would

A shin dagger, below, is
part of the desert's
fascinating botanical
assemblage.

repay the government's investment over a period of years. In 1903, they formed the Salt River Valley Water Users' Association, parent of the Salt River Project, the entity that still delivers water and electric power to a million Phoenicians.

Once the political machinations were ironed out, the physical realities of the ambitious construction project had to be confronted. At the dam site, there was nothing but a river running through hot desert and four regal mountain peaks standing watch.

Native stone came in handy as the basic material from which the dam would be built. Hauling cement was an expensive proposition, so a mortar plant was built nearby. Wood came from a sawmill in the Sierra Ancha, the highlands east of the Tonto Basin.

Thousands came in to help build the dam — stone masons, loggers, and wranglers; Apache, African-American, Mexican, and European — earning $2.50 to $5 a day. Many lived with their families in tents in the original town of Roosevelt, now under the waters.

The Salt River's unpredictable rises delayed construction, and the dam ended up running several million dollars over budget. When the last chiseled stone was set in February 1911, Roosevelt Dam and related projects had cost a hefty $10 million. Its graceful masonry curve rose 284 feet above the bed of the river. Behind it stretched Roosevelt Lake, then the largest artificial lake in the world, storing 1.3 million acre-feet of water. Deliveries of that water

A diverse plant mix, above — piñon pine, cottonwood and oak trees, manzanita shrubs, and sotol — grows in the mid-elevations of Four Peaks and the neighboring Sierra Ancha. When the desert decides to put on a wildflower show, following pages, it pulls out all the stops. Mexican poppies, gilia, and a cast of thousands splash the flanks of Stewart Mountain near Saguaro Lake. Such springtime flowering results from good winter rains.

Water performs magic in the desert. It flows and sculpts, rages and whispers. Rising in the White Mountains where the Black and White rivers come together, Arizona's Salt River, above, carves canyons and carries mountains, one cobble at a time, to the sea.

would irrigate more than 200,000 acres of land. On the afternoon of March 18, former President Theodore Roosevelt dedicated the dam that bore his name. At the celebration, TR told the assembled crowd, "You could not have done anything that would have pleased and touched me more than to name this great dam after me."

To get other materials to the dam site, a wagon road had been built from Mesa, the nearest railhead. Between 1903 and 1905, some 60 miles of curvaceous dirt roadway was hewn in the tight space between the Salt River and the rugged Superstition Mountains. Freighters coaxed heavy, mule-drawn wagons along its sidewinder path, up and down the 10 percent grade of famous Fish Creek Hill and around hairpin curves, stopping at watering stations and changing teams three times during the 10-hour trip.

While it served as the supply route for the dam, the Mesa-Roosevelt road immediately attracted tourists in search of views and thrills. In the first year the road was open, the first automobile — a 14-passenger Knox called the

Rounded edges and smoothness are the tell-tale signs of rock, below, that's been washed by a river for ages.

"Red Terror" — made the run to Roosevelt in an hour and a half. Daredevil drivers delighted in trying to beat that record, sharing the right-of-way with 20 to 60 freight teams a day.

A small album in the archives of the Arizona State University library contains sepia-toned photographs by H.C. Tibbitts. Embossed in gold leaf on the album's brown leather cover is the title "Apache Trail: The Wonder Trip through Oldest America." The photos were taken to illustrate a 1916 *Sunset* magazine article by writer Walter Woehlke. According to historian Pat Stein, that article coined the term Apache Trail, the name by which the amazing route is still known today. In 1991, graduate student William Packard rephotographed Tibbitts' shots from exactly the same locations. The changes, and in some cases the lack thereof, are fascinating. The original shots show Apache Indians at their brush wickiups beside the new lake, a free-flowing Salt River below Roosevelt Dam, and the Apache Trail, then all dirt, leading to it. Between

Water exposed and carved the granite bed of Salome Creek, below. In hidden places, water lingers on in natural pockets in the rock, like polished gems in the desert.

1920 and 1946, the three additional lakes downstream of Roosevelt were built, power lines were strung across the country, bridges were improved, and portions of the Apache Trail were realigned, widened, and paved. After 1991, Roosevelt Dam was raised 77 feet and its beautiful cut masonry refaced with a plain facade. Now, the lake can hold an additional half-million acre-feet of water. And rather than crossing on the crest of the dam, motorists now drive over a blue bridge that arches across the lake.

We leave the highway along Tonto Creek and wind up to Four Peaks on a dirt road past saguaro cactus and creosote bush, through evergreen oaks,

Plants and animals rely on hidden water in Salome Creek, right, when the rest of the desert runs dry.

The west face of the Superstition Mountains, below, looks toward the Valley of the Sun.

manzanita, and finally into ponderosa. At Lone Pine Saddle, it is possible to join Four Peaks and Browns Peak trails. The rugged face of Browns Peak, the highest of the four summits, rises to 7,600 feet above sea level; several people have described the hands-and-knees scramble involved in reaching the top. In 1996, a forest fire scorched nearly 60,000 acres here in the heart of Four Peaks Wilderness. Blackened deadfall has turned the trails into obstacle courses, forcing us to step over and bend under downed trees every few feet. We camp at the saddle that night in a howling wind. Given the breeze and the trail conditions, we decide to scuttle plans for the bushwhack up Browns Peak, rationalizing that this is the time of year to be down enjoying the desert rather than shivering on a blustery mountain top.

We end up the next night high on a cliff in the Sierra Ancha, and again a gale rocks the camper until we fear its collapse. Finally we surrender, moving two more times to lower, more sheltered locales. We awake beside the Salt River, content to while away the morning there.

The Superstitions stand as a formidable wall just east of Phoenix. To get supplies to the site of Roosevelt Dam, the Apache Trail had to traverse intimidating terrain like Fish Creek Hill, left.

Agave stalks flit across the silhouette of Four Peaks like moths at sunset. The summits' profile is imprinted on our vision of Arizona.

Nothing holds more promise than a river in early morning as the sun slips up over canyon walls, lighting and warming the world. I find a comfortable boulder for a backrest and nestle in, luxuriating like a lizard in that blessed warmth. A downstream wind whistles in the bridge girders, waves the grasses by the shore, and ruffles the surface of the water. I watch for signs of life to bob up in the silken, green water.

I remember this place on a dark Sunday night a number of years ago as I waited for Michael and our friends to arrive after an adventuresome boat trip through upper Salt River Canyon. On the trip we witnessed firsthand the transformation of this desert river into its spring flood stage — a river not in parentheses on any map. We had been on the water only a day before awakening to the tick-tick-tick of snow striking the roof of our nylon tent. Peering outside, I was greeted by the incongruous sight of saguaro cactus frosted with white. It had been raining and snowing all night; we stood on the bank and watched in near disbelief as the river turned into a fearsome brown maelstrom. The water flow rose from a modest 2,000 cubic feet a second to just under 10,000 cfs. Without getting overly technical, what that meant was the trip was scuttled for the passengers. It was too cold and too dangerous for all of us to continue downstream unprepared for such conditions. After lengthy debate, the five boatmen acknowledged they had to row the boats down, while the passengers would hike back out along the road to the put-in point.

As we separated, we prayed to the river gods for those who were headed into the stream's maw. Walking out, in comparison, seemed like a reprieve — until we came to the first side stream. It was a murky red torrent, brimming

Autumn comes to the Four Peaks region in unexpected ways. The crimson of bigtooth maple leaves envelopes the atmosphere of deep desert canyons and weaves a carpet of color at one's feet.

bank to bank with water and flashing full-bore towards the river. We'd have to ford on foot with no sure idea of its true depth. After plenty of hemming and hawing, one of our troop stepped out with great care. The rest of us followed, making it across safely. But as we proceeded, we wondered how many more such crossings would be necessary before reaching the vehicles. However, the rest was uneventful. We spent the remainder of the weekend in Globe, warm and dry, wondering with occasional guilt how our cohorts were faring.

On Sunday we headed to the take-out and waited all afternoon for the boats to arrive. As dusk settled in, we started to get a little anxious. As it got darker, that uneasiness turned to genuine concern. Where were they? Had something happened at Quartzite Falls, the notorious rapid that normally required a laborious portage to get around? We were most keenly aware of the diversion dam just below the take-out, a place that had claimed the lives of inexperienced boaters a few years earlier. We knew our compadres would exercise extreme caution and avoid this hazard at all cost. As these dire thoughts swam through our minds, we saw flickers of flashlights and heard voices. They'd made it! And rather than going to the usual take-out ramp, they pulled in at the cliff. Derigging in the dark took several hours, scrambling and hoisting heavy gear, including inflated rafts, up the rocky slope. They reported a wild ride. One boat had to be patched after a run-in with a sharp rock, and the river was so high and so fast that for uncomfortably long stretches they had no hope of pulling over.

Here I am, sitting by that same cliff where that river trip ended, memories of that adventure balanced against the peacefulness of this morning. Like that Colorado cowboy, I love to see old pictures. They tell me stories about human determination and faith. But the river tells me things too — of bald eagles perched on desert shores, of mountain waters gathering, of a force more powerful than all our feeble attempts at control. ❧

White Mountains

White Mountains

A Sense of Being Within

In the summer of 1909, a bright young forester fresh out of Yale made the 2-day wagon trip from the railhead in Holbrook to the headquarters of the newly created Apache National Forest in the White Mountains of eastern Arizona. His name was Aldo Leopold.

On horseback, Leopold spent his first summer mapping and cruising timber in the lush forests. Referring to the region in the singular, he declared that this "White Mountain" was a "horseman's world. . . . the county-sized plateau known as 'on top' was the exclusive domain of the mounted man: mounted cowman, mounted sheepman, mounted forest officer, mounted trapper, and those unclassified mounted men of unknown origin and uncertain destination always found on frontiers."

Aldo Leopold rose rapidly through the ranks of the fledgling Forest Service and led the choir in the song for protection of game species like deer and wild turkey. The way to do that, he and others believed, was to have fewer mountain lions, grizzly bears, and wolves.

Graduating from greenhorn to guru of America's land-preservation movement, Leopold began to express his growing ecological consciousness

The White Mountains contribute graceful meadows and high lakes to Arizona. Crescent and Big lakes, preceding pages, lure anglers from around the state. The stunning gold of aspen in autumn cloaks Escudilla Mountain, left.

49

Early cattle and sheep ranchers were drawn to the fertile Round Valley and the White Mountains. The hills around Springerville are ancient volcanoes, their edges now softened by a carpet of grass.

in eloquent prose. In an essay titled "Thinking Like a Mountain," he reveals a transforming experience when he and other hunters shot an old wolf in the rimrock country. Upon reaching the dying animal, he saw "a fierce green fire dying her eyes."

He continued, "I realized then, and have known ever since, that there was something new to me in those eyes — something known only to her and to the mountain. I was young then, and full of trigger-itch; I thought that because fewer wolves meant more deer, that no wolves would mean hunter's paradise. But after seeing the green fire die, I sensed that neither the wolf nor the mountain agreed with such a view."

For Aldo Leopold, the White Mountains were paradise. They remain so today. But they're different from most mountains. The first and lasting impression is that a person is not so much *on* these mountains as *in* them. Their summits and knolls and domes roll away in the distance like big, blue ocean

breakers. They cradle immense meadows, grass-filled bowls brightened in summer with harebell, primrose, and daisy. Kestrels hover over exhilarating expanses of golden grama grass, and herds of elk flow across the meadows like brown rivers. The drooping branches of spike-topped spruce rim the meadow coves, an alpine forest of gnomes and elves. Small lakes and moist cienegas fill the swales. At dusk, bugs hatch, fish rise, and ospreys hunt over the silver waters.

Names of places in these mountains write a vibrant history and bespeak the bond between landscape and language: Firebox Lake, Boardshack Knoll, Dutch Oven Spring. Wildcat Point, Gobbler Peak, Skunk Flat, Bear Wallow. Willow Creek, Raspberry Peak, Rosebud Cienega. Boneyard Creek, Profanity Ridge, and Moonshine Peak.

These mountains are the homeland of White Mountain and San Carlos Apache Indians. And though their place names appear less frequently on

Inscrutable artwork created by Ancestral Pueblo people embellishes basalt boulders, below.

maps, the Apache know them well. Translated into English, those place names show a close particularity with the land: Descending to Water (where a sandstone cliff is next to a spring), Gray Willows Curve Around a Bend (by a stream), and Trail Extends Across Scorched Rocks (at a canyon crossing).

Beyond simple description, the names of places hold great import. As Apache Dudley Patterson told anthropologist Keith Basso, "Wisdom sits in places.... You must remember everything about them. You must learn their names, you must remember what happened at them long ago."

In their highest reaches, the White Mountains are the natal home of the headwaters of several of Arizona's most important rivers. The Little Colorado River rises from a spring on Mount Baldy — at 11,590 feet, the second-highest point in the state. The East and West forks join into a defined Little Colorado, which flows north and west to join the main stem Colorado deep in the Grand Canyon. The Black, the White, and the Blue rivers are born in these mountains too. At Three Forks, a trio of tributaries meets and enters a steep-walled rocky canyon as the Black River gains force. It meets the White deep in Apacheland, and together the two weave southwestward to form the Salt River. The Blue River begins in the Sierra Azul, or Blue Range, on the east side of the White Mountains, then heads south to add its waters to the Gila.

These rivers have always served as pathways. Hungry grizzly bears once emerged from their dens in spring and prowled the river banks in search of fresh, green growth. People followed the rivers too. In the 1200s, Mogollon folk built a big pueblo among the terraces of a basalt-capped mesa overlooking Round Valley on the Little Colorado at the present-day town of Springerville. Spanish settlers called it Casa Malpais — "House of the Badlands" — and for a century, archaeologists have puzzled over the site's open courtyard, large square kiva-like structure, a possible astronomical "observatory," and rooms hidden in deep rock chambers.

Earliest Spanish entrants, on a vain quest for fabled cities of gold, followed the rivers north through the mountains. In June 1540, Francisco Vázquez de Coronado and his entourage, traveling north from Mexico, rested 2 days at Black River Crossing, then went on to the White River. They named it the "River of Rafts" because they had to build boats there to get their supplies across.

Apache weavers gathered river-grown willow, sumac, and cottonwood

Ancestral Puebloans built a large community at Casa Malpais, left, northeast of present-day Springerville.

As summer gives way
to autumn, below,
monsoon storms give
way to softer rains.

for their exquisite burden baskets and twined water carriers. Crusty trappers sought marketable beaver pelts along the streams. Basque sheepherders and Anglo ranchers found the well-watered highlands ideal summer grazing grounds for sheep and cattle. Mining companies acquired and traded the water in the river basins, then sluiced it down to copper mines in southern Arizona. And Mormon settlers laid out tidy towns at Greer, Eagar, Springerville, St. Johns, and Snowflake. They too diverted the water of the rivers and streams to their fields and gristmills.

The West Fork of the Little Colorado tumbles off Mount Baldy as a burbling mountain brook. Fallen logs span its shallow 4-foot width. Leggy yellow sneezeweed sparks the grassy banks. Springs spill off the hillsides, crowded with deep pink and crimson checkermallow, thistle, and wild rose. Trout flash through the water, prey of many an angler who has tried to lure

Along Paddy Creek on
the south flank of
Escudilla Mountain,
left, the delicate leaves
of quaking aspen turn
from green to gold
in a breathtaking
transformation. A
tunnel of color,
following pages, leads
hikers up Toolbox Draw
to the top of Escudilla.

them with a hooked worm. Rock squirrels rasp at intruders, and nervous chickadees flit through the tree branches like salesmen working a crowd.

On an idyllic July morning, a group of Apache school children from White-river hiked up the West Fork trail into the Mount Baldy Wilderness. They carried their lunches in white plastic grocery bags, and clutched wildflower and mushroom field guides. An elder Apache woman trudged past us, while a younger woman stopped to talk. We knew that the summit of Mount Baldy was closed to entry to anyone except Apaches. It is one of their most sacred places, home of amiable spirits called *gaan*. When I asked the young woman what the mountain meant to her, she paused for a moment, then answered: "It feels really good to be up there. I pray and leave offerings and look for colored beads."

White beads are especially treasured. They are for the girls, she explained. Turquoise beads are for boys.

I recalled another momentous pilgrimage made by an Arizona man years ago. In 1982, photographer Nick Berezenko walked the entire length of the Little Colorado River. On rented plastic snowshoes, Nick carried his pack over 4-foot-deep snowfields on Baldy, where he spent the night.

The next morning he greeted sunrise on the rock-rubbled peak in knife-sharp winds, and there began his epic journey. From the first drops of melting water, he followed the river as closely as he could, down the West Fork, past the village of Greer and the towns of Springerville, St. Johns, and Woodruff, his progress slowed by fences, quicksand, and clots of tamarisk. Along the way, he met some Navajo and descendants of the region's Mormon pioneers. Most of all, he says, he learned the "life history . . . the many personalities" of this river that begins as a small, clear mountain stream, becomes a wide, ephemeral desert wash, and ends in aquamarine blue between the towering gorge walls just before entering the mother stream in Grand Canyon.

I met Nick completely by chance at a most unlikely place. I was with a group on a Colorado River rafting trip in Grand Canyon. We had waded up the Little Colorado a few miles, and there he sat, perched on a lip of rock, smiling broadly. Despite a leak in his canary yellow air mattress that he'd brought to hold his gear as he navigated deep pools, he was about to complete a 36-day, 329-mile walk that few, if any, have ever done. We walked back to the boats together, and Nick happily accepted a ride downstream the next

morning. We dropped him off at the base of the Tanner Trail, with a cold beer in his hand, and waved goodbye.

"I got to know that river," he said of the Little Colorado, a statement he'd certainly earned the right to make.

A century earlier, a vanguard of Mormon colonists traveled in the opposite direction, *up* the Little Colorado. Obeying the call of Church of Jesus Christ of Latter-day Saints leader Brigham Young, the vanguard left southern Utah, crossed the Colorado at Lees Ferry, traversed the Painted Desert, and founded Sunset, Obed, Brigham City, and other settlements along the Little Colorado in northeastern Arizona. The cantankerous river, though, fought them at

every turn. Repeatedly, it flooded out the dams the settlers had erected across its path. A few of the settlements lasted, most did not.

One that did survive was the town of Snowflake. In 1877, William Flake sold all his worldly possessions and set out from southern Utah. With him was one of his wives, Lucy Hannah Flake, who nursed their daughters when they contracted diphtheria during the trip. The following year, Flake bought a ranch in the Silver Creek Valley, a tributary of the Little Colorado at the edge of the White Mountains, and along with fellow churchman Erastus Snow founded the community of Snowflake, combining their surnames.

On occasion, the hard life of the frontier tested Lucy's faith. When she felt "depressed in her spirits," she went to her sister's and they poured out their souls in a "glorious feast of prair [sic]." Today, Mormon heritage is strong and thriving in Snowflake and other White Mountain towns. Church bishops keep close tabs on teenagers in their wards. Steadfast Saints still squirrel away a year's worth of corn in their garages, and they proudly escort visitors through the stout brick homes built by their grandparents. And in the year

The East Fork of Black River, below, flows south of Big Lake. In the Big Lake area, following pages, aspen trees, baneberry, and lichen-covered rocks provide some of the decor.

2001, the church completed construction of a temple in Snowflake — only the second in Arizona — the place where the most sacred Mormon ceremonies are conducted.

Non-Mormons were attracted to the White Mountains too, among them brothers Gustav and Julius Becker, freighters and merchants who came to Springerville in 1876. In the back of the Becker store on Main Street was the drug department. According to Ed Becker, "Gustav…had a big German doctor book, which he used to diagnose the ailments of people who came to him. He used the mortar and pestle to grind his own medicines." With the dearth of doctors in the area, people around St. Johns often called on the woman known as Aunt Charlotte. As R. Keith Udall recollected, she was known "by every man, woman and child in St. Johns, for she carried a little black doctor's bag which contained medicine and instruments to bring babies, relieve fever, bandage wounds, splint broken bones." Aunt Charlotte midwifed somewhere between 500 and 1,000 babies in her 30 years of practice.

Not so long ago, the White Mountains were still upholding a reputation

The White Mountains
are a big land seasoned
with infinite details.
Above, a sunset bursts
over Rudd Knoll.

as part of the Wild West. There were your run-of-the-mill stampedes, shootings, roundups, and rustlings. Famed lawmen, like Commodore Perry Owens, the Apache County sheriff, tried to keep the peace. They rode herd on notorious outlaws such as the Blevins Gang and minor miscreants such as Pat Trainor. When asked, during one of his many appearances before the judge in St. Johns, whether he pled guilty or not guilty, Trainor replied, "That yet remains to be proven." There was even the occasional murder, as attested by a wooden grave marker, adorned with plastic flowers, along a forest road near the East Fork of the Black River. Carved into the marker are these words: OSCAR SHULTZ SHOT MAY 17 1922.

Local resident Weg Sharp recalled clearly just what happened to poor Oscar. He had held up some tourists on their way into the valley, but the $4.50 Oscar netted wasn't worth his while. Still, the victims reported the incident to the sheriff in St. Johns, who set out with a posse. For some unknown

Below, a coneflower is a sign of summer along the East Fork of the Black River. On the following pages, velvet waters at sunset invite reflection at Crescent Lake.

reason, Oscar had turned his horse loose and was on foot when the enforcers came upon him. He managed to confiscate the sheriff's horse and ride off, ending up at Nutrioso for a night. Still on the lam, Oscar took refuge up in a tree and watched as the posse rode right underneath him. He then proceeded to hold up the bank in McNary, which yielded more than a hundred dollars.

"He wanted the money to send his mother," declared Sharp, but this time the posse followed him and killed him.

Now the White Mountains are becoming known for another kind of wildness, of the natural kind. In fact, they've been identified by The Nature Conservancy as a "hot spot" of species diversity in the ecoregion that spans the border of eastern Arizona and western New Mexico. As a beginning in their efforts to protect and restore the riches, the organization purchased Sierra Blanca Ranch, just west of the small town of Alpine, in the summer of 2000.

Perennial streams, springs, and wetlands there, in the headwaters of the Black River, harbor Apache trout, Arizona's state fish, and the threatened loach minnow, along with the rare Chiricahua leopard frog and a freshwater mussel called (no kidding) the California floater, the only one of its kind in Arizona.

Beyond the aquatic species, the White Mountains were also the final stronghold of large carnivores. Biologist David Brown discovered records indicating that Arizona's last known grizzly bear was killed on Mount Baldy in 1939. And while a few wolves remained along the Black River on Apache land, they were largely gone from the White Mountains as early as 1920. In a concerted campaign, both animals were hunted and trapped to protect livestock from their depredations.

At left, ponderosa and aspen above Greer welcome winter. And at Sierra Blanca Lake, following pages, the echo of howling wolves once again resounds.

69

A lone ponderosa pine, below, seems to signify the remoteness of the White Mountains northeast of Crescent Lake.

But now, the haunting howls of wolves — and the green fire in their eyes — again live in the White Mountains. In 1998, within a mile of the place where young Aldo Leopold watched that old wolf die, the first Mexican gray wolves were released from holding pens in a highly publicized project to reintroduce these animals to their native ground. Some 30 wolves roam the Blue Range and other locations in the White Mountains. It may be a long time before their numbers triple, as biologists and wolf advocates hope. We are only beginning to learn what is known to these animals and to these mountains. ∾

Delicate leaves of potentilla, left, cover a portion of the ground at KP Cienega, a marshy area near 9,000 feet elevation.

Huachuca Mountains

Huachuca Mountains

A Piñata of Treats

It's Easter Sunday in Garden Canyon in southeastern Arizona's Huachuca Mountains. A few families have arrived early to get a picnic table. Michael and I drive up the road as far as we can go, then get out and start walking. In about a half-mile, we see a trio of women crouched low, scanning the trees along the creek. They've spotted something, so we keep our voices down and, ever so subtly, join in their discovery.

"There he is!" they exclaim, training their binoculars on the branches of a large, white-barked sycamore. The object of their excitement is a bird. We hear the weird call, like a barking dog, the sound of a male elegant trogon. Decked out in beautiful green back, red breast, and long coppery tail, he adds an exotic touch of the subtropical here. Michael had never seen this splendid bird, and this was only my second sighting. I'm thrilled with our good fortune so early in the day.

Bird-watchers know Garden Canyon as a reliable place to see elegant trogons. Garden and a few other canyons in neighboring mountains are the only places in the United States where it's possible to do so. Elegant trogons come into southeastern Arizona in the spring to breed and nest in

The Huachuca Mountains rise against the Mexican border in southeastern Arizona, a geographical position that heavily influences the region's biological and cultural riches. On the west side of the Huachucas, the San Rafael Valley, preceding pages, holds the headwaters of the Santa Cruz River. The Mule Mountains, left, wind north from Bisbee above the San Pedro River.

cavities in mature sycamore trees. They stay through the summer, stuffing big juicy insects into the mouths of their young, then head south in the fall.

All of this I learned recently, but my infatuation with trogons dates back 20 years when a friend and I hiked up Mount Wrightson in the Santa Rita Mountains. He thought he heard one in a canyon, and I took him at his word. For me bird-watching has been like some other endeavors in life — trying to learn a foreign language and playing a musical instrument. It takes virtues of patience and discipline that I seem to lack. Still, I never forgot his description of the bird, which was then called the coppery-tailed trogon.

Two decades later, I set out on a more concerted search for trogons in the mountains of southeastern Arizona. I came in August, the time of year when the Huachucas are in an avian frenzy. First stop was The Nature Conservancy preserve in Ramsey Canyon. Though trogons were on my mind, I was enthralled to watch hummingbirds of every size and color zinging through the air, along with painted redstarts and sulphur-bellied flycatchers. I continued eastward to the Chiricahua Mountains, to the South Fork of Cave Creek, prime trogon territory. It was midday and so hot that I feigned rapt interest in every bird-sized cavity in every sycamore I passed, if only because the trees provided welcome shade. I soon realized that no self-respecting trogon would be active at that time of day.

Finally, as my late summer birding tour of southeastern Arizona was ending, I backtracked to Madera Canyon in the Santa Ritas south of Tucson. There, as I watched hummingbirds at the lodge feeders, I ever so casually inquired of an Indiana visitor whether he'd seen any trogons.

"Oh sure," he said. "There's a nest right up the canyon, about a hundred yards off the trail. You can't miss it."

I beelined up there and sat down near a sycamore that matched the bird-watcher's description. Within 10 minutes, a flash of color cruised through the tree canopy. It was a trogon, a male flying in with immense insects in its bill and stuffing them into the cavity that held two hungry nestlings calling impatiently for dad to deliver lunch. Perfectly still and breathless, I watched as he returned a second, a third, and finally a fourth time, bearing the trogon version of fast food.

One of Mexico's contributions to southeastern Arizona is the San Pedro River, one of the few rivers in North America to flow northward. The San Pedro's green thread, right, marks the course of the river as it meanders near Hereford. Cottonwoods, following pages, form an arching canopy at the San Pedro Riparian National Conservation Area east of Sierra Vista.

A sunflower, below, decorates The Nature Conservancy's Patagonia-Sonoita Creek Preserve.

After our Garden Canyon visit, I revisit Ramsey Canyon and go for a walk with Nature Conservancy naturalist Mark Pretti. Mark has difficulty finishing a sentence, because just as he's talking about a new hummingbird that's zipped in (he's already tallied five hummingbird species), he stops and gasps at the season's first sight of a butterfly called a "sister." Oh, and then he spies a pair of painted redstarts, and a dusky-capped flycatcher, "a little bit of the tropics."

Elegant trogons. Lucifer hummingbirds. Yellow-billed cuckoos. Gray hawks. Barking frogs. Long-nosed bats. Coatimundis. Coues white-tailed deer. Jaguars. Water umbels. Lemon lilies. All these animals and plants make the Huachuca Mountains a piñata of biological treats. The Huachucas and neighboring mountains of southeast Arizona — the Chiricahuas, Santa Ritas, Dragoons, Whetstones, Mustangs, and Mules — are known as "sky islands." From a distance they seem to float like dark green, wooded islands out of oceans of desert and grassland. Because of each range's isolation, and the inability of some animals to cross those valley barriers, species tend to specialize: The handsome Apache red squirrel is restricted to the Chiricahuas; the Arizona gray squirrel is in the Huachucas and Santa Ritas; and the endangered Mount Graham red squirrel lives only at the top of the Pinalenos.

These sky islands form part of an "archipelago" of nearly 40 mountain ranges in the borderlands (including Arizona, New Mexico, and Mexico). Though other sky-island complexes exist in the Great Basin, Venezuela, and Africa, this southwestern assemblage stands out, say biologists, because it is the only one that extends from subtropical to temperate latitudes.

Adding to this tantalizing tapestry of life are canyons — Garden, Ramsey, Miller, and Carr — that slash down the rugged east side of the heavy-browed Huachucas. Nearly all of them host year-round streams lined with deciduous trees like Arizona walnut, sycamore, ash, and bigtooth maple. These canyons provide the most accessible approach into the mountains and serve as sanctuary for even more species. Here scientists first found the Ramsey Canyon leopard frog, known since the 1980s but described as a new species only in 1993. Their formal name, *Rana subaquavocalis*, refers to the habit of the males of singing underwater to attract mates.

I got a good, closeup look at these big spotted frogs in ponds at the Beattys' in Miller Canyon. Under nearly complete natural camouflage, these frogs perch on their haunches on floating lily pads, half in the water and

Hundreds of years ago, Spanish land grants in the San Rafael Valley, east of Nogales, claimed this prime grazing country, left. These grasses at the base of the Patagonia Mountains still nourish a ranching way of life. The valley, following pages, stretches into Mexico.

The Huachucas, above, are one of several isolated mountain ranges in southeastern Arizona known as "sky islands," for the way they seem to float out of the surrounding desert. The San Pedro River weaves through the desert on the range's east side, providing a migratory corridor for hundreds of bird species.

half out, eyes bulging straight ahead. Should a menacing shadow move over them, their true numbers are revealed as they catapult in unison off their pads and into the water.

The healthy population of rare leopard frogs is only one attraction at Tom and Edith Beatty's place, tucked beneath 9,466-foot Miller Peak, the highest point in the Huachucas. They tend a fruit orchard, and Edith raises chickens, bees, and the best rhubarb this side of the Mississippi. The eggs, honey, and rhubarb are for sale at an outdoor table, and payment is on the honor system. The Beattys also maintain an array of hummingbird feeders that attract birders from spring through summer. Conversation at the dinner table centers on Tom's latest project — building a guest house that's "off the grid" — his elk-hunting success, a rare sighting of a short-tailed hawk, and reports of Mexican wolves only 5 miles across the border.

86

Early people who passed this way left pictographs, below, like these in Garden Canyon.

Immediately beyond the confines of narrow stream corridors like Miller Canyon, a drier, rockier environment dominates these mountains. The steep slopes are thickly clothed with agave, bear grass, manzanita, sumac, a perplexing number of stiff-leaved evergreen oaks, and four different kinds of pines. The forests resemble those in the Sierra Madre in Mexico. Where this so-called Madrean woodland spills into southern Arizona, it meets three other major natural communities — the Rocky Mountains at their farthest southern extent and two major North American deserts, the Sonoran and the Chihuahuan, overlapping from west and east.

With elements from all four big biomes coming together and mixing, biologists proclaim this sky-island region to be "a center of mega-diversity" on the planet.

One mephitic mammal illustrates this great confluence. Only in the

The northwest edge of the Chihuahuan Desert reaches into the Huachuca Mountains region of Arizona. High grasslands and soaptree yucca, below, near the Mustang Mountains, distinguish the Chihuahuan from the saguaro-filled Sonoran Desert.

Cottonwoods, right, signal the presence of underground water in Cochise Stronghold in the Dragoon Mountains, northeast of the Huachucas.

Southwest's sky islands do four species of skunks — striped, spotted, hooded, and hog-nosed — occur in one place.

Flowing north out of Mexico on the east side of the Huachucas stretches a band of liquid green, the San Pedro River. Michael and I stroll along the sandy banks of the slow-moving stream in April, when so many caterpillars inhabit the cottonwoods that we literally hear them munching. We notice a "serious" bird-watcher peering in a spotting scope and thumbing through his field guide. As I tiptoe by, he asks if I know my warblers. He's spied one that appears different from anything he can find in his book. I advise that he's talking to an ornithologically challenged person, but I'm game to take a look. While we ponder the mystery bird, he points out a Wilson's warbler, a flash

Aspens, below, gild the
north side of Carr Peak,
second-highest summit
in the Huachucas.

of pure gold amid the emerald cottonwood leaves. I nod in knowing agreement when he suggests the other, problematic bird may be just a yellow-
rumped warbler that doesn't match the pictures in the field guide. With
more than 380 species of birds — millions of individuals — living here or
passing through, the San Pedro has earned the title of "Globally Important
Bird Area."

In the riverside San Pedro House, a gift shop and bookstore, T-shirts celebrate the reintroduction of beavers in 1999. The work of these industrious
rodents was responsible for the cienegas, or swampy wetlands, that were
strung up and down the river a century ago.

These wetlands, writes Roseann Hanson, were the "defining riparian habitat type" along the San Pedro. The beaver were trapped out, and the marshes
were drained because of worry about malaria-carrying mosquitoes. But
today, beavers are back and doing well. Their natural proclivities may help
restore cienegas and kick-start ecological recovery all along the river.

It's hard to know whether Francisco Vázquez de Coronado noticed beavers
along the San Pedro. In 1540, then only 30 years old, Coronado was appointed
by Viceroy Antonio de Mendoza to lead a monumental expedition north
from Mexico into New Spain's frontier. Under his charge were more than
300 cavalrymen and soldiers, wives and children, 800 Indians, a handful of
priests, and an unknown number of black slaves, along with pack animals,
sheep, cattle, and goats numbering in the thousands.

Coronado's main goal was to find Cíbola, the Seven Cities of Gold; while
pursuing that aim, the conquistador always sent an advance guard march-
ing ahead, bearing a cross as a sign of peace to the indigenous people. But
by August of 1540, after nearly 6 months of grueling travel across the interior,
the strain was starting to show. Exhausted from the difficult terrain and lack
of food, they arrived, according to Captain Jaramillo, "at an arroyo which we
understand was called Nexpa," the river most historians believe was the San
Pedro in present-day Arizona. Indians, likely Sobaipuri, met them and shared
roasted agave leaves and cactus fruits.

Eventually Coronado went as far as Quivira in what is now central Kansas,
but his expedition was ultimately considered a failure. Though this was the
first fully documented group of Europeans to enter the Southwest, the cities
of gold were nothing but rumor. And Coronado's later encounters with other

Miller Peak, at 9,466
feet, left, is the highest
point in the Huachuca
Mountains. Autumn
colors have already
tinged the aspen and
maples near the top,
while agave stalks
spike the grassy hills at
lower elevations.

native people were not nearly as pleasant as those along the San Pedro.

Still, large Spanish land grants were carved into this part of the country. Spaniards established missions and presidios, brought in livestock, and unearthed silver. For 300 years, the land south of the Gila River, what we know as southern Arizona, was a part of New Spain. Then, it belonged to Mexico for a time. After 2 years of war, Mexico and the United States signed the Treaty of Guadalupe Hidalgo in 1848. The international boundary was established, but not finalized until the Gadsden Treaty of 1853 settled the dispute over the land south of the Gila. That final agreement, writes land historian Robert Humphrey, "was not the result of an amicable afternoon spent over a cup of tea or even a few bottles of Mexican beer."

The United States' effort at surveying the boundary, from the Gulf of Mexico to the Pacific Ocean, started under boundary commissioner John Russell Bartlett, a politician. Later, Maj. William Emory, a topographical engineer,

From mid-October to late November, bigtooth and Rocky Mountain maples, left, spangle stream sides in the Huachucas' Miller Canyon. In the neighboring Chiricahua Mountains, fallen maple leaves temporarily rest on moss- and lichen-covered boulders, above.

Miller Creek nourishes a multitude of life, from minute forms to residents of a town miles away. Below, an infusion of sycamore and maple leaves provides food for stream-dwelling organisms.

Some water is withdrawn from the creek, right, and piped across the San Pedro River to the town of Tombstone.

assumed leadership. As the line was charted, crude piles of rocks were laid up to mark the boundary. With the survey long done, Major Emory then took on the task of seeing that permanent monuments were put in place at intervals along the international boundary. In 3 years, 258 of the structures were installed — each weighed 710 pounds (some were of stone, others of iron) — and were hauled in by wagon or on mules. A few still stand at the south end of the Huachucas.

With Emory came botanist and geologist Dr. Charles C. Parry, who commented when they arrived in the San Pedro Valley that "The country here begins to assume most attractive features. To the north and west rise high

Maple leaves, below, bear fall colors.

mountain ridges clothed with pine and oak groves; the intervening country is everywhere carpeted with fine grama grass.... Water is frequent in the valleys."

At 7,000 feet on Coronado Peak at the far south end of the Huachucas, the view takes in two neighboring nations, a line drawn by men and now reinforced by a fence, showing the world where one stops and the other begins. But from this view, looking down 2,000 feet into the valley, the land is of a whole piece — the green ribbon of the San Pedro River obeys no international boundary, neither do the trogons in search of nests, nor the blue mountains standing like islands in their midst. ∾

Spreading sycamores with ghostly white bark, left, are the chosen homes of elegant trogons, birds found stateside only in the Huachucas and a few other sky-island ranges in southeastern Arizona.

97

Kofa Mountains

Kofa Mountains

Where Extremes Abound

Arizona abounds in extremes, and nowhere are those extremes more pronounced than in the state's southwestern corner. In this far reach, within 15 miles of each other, rise the sunstruck face of the Kofa Mountains and the satin-soft waters of the Colorado River, the region's starkest desert and the Southwest's mother stream.

The sighting of a waterbird on a January day vividly illustrates this disparity.

We were out in our little fishing boat on Martinez Lake on the Colorado. Michael killed the motor and rowed quietly into a marshy cove, crammed with American coots mewing like kittens as they paddled around. Handsome in gray, black, and white, these birds look like they're dressed for a formal dinner. A double-crested cormorant perched on a snag, flaring its wings to dry its feathers. A congregation of white pelicans clung close to shore, turning their backs on us as we entered their personal space. A large bird, flying fast toward us on a glide slope, captured our attention. By the size and light color, we first thought it was an osprey. The bird's presence rattled the calm of the coots, but they weren't the object of its attention. In one clean swift

The mountains of Arizona's southwestern corner consist mostly of bare rock and blistering desert. The Colorado River, preceding pages, cuts between the Trigo and Chocolate mountains as it rolls through the Imperial National Wildlife Refuge. A barrel cactus, left, glows as the last light of sunset washes up against the Castle Dome Mountains.

The waters of the Colorado River are stilled above Imperial Dam north of Yuma. Backwaters along Martinez and Ferguson lakes offer diverse habitat for plants and animals. Some plants, below, are salt-loving.

Plants along the waters, right, offer fine nesting for multitudes of birds.

plunge, the big bird dove into the water, nailed a small silver fish, then skimmed away low over the surface, gobbling its catch en route.

Through binoculars, I noted the forked tail and cayenne-colored bill. Michael guessed it was a tern. Checking the bird list and my field guide, I discovered that the size and bill color suggested a Caspian tern, a winter migrant to the lower Colorado from northern climes. The biologist at the Imperial National Wildlife Refuge confirmed that they had been reported.

That spellbinding sighting contrasts with one on another winter day, up in the Castle Dome Mountains northeast of the river. We'd been camping and poking around the old mines and ghost towns. We tentatively tested our truck's four-wheel drive as we crawled through McPherson Pass. Desert bighorn sheep are the trademark animals of the Castle Domes and next-door Kofa Mountains — the main reason these ranges were incorporated into the Kofa National Wildlife Refuge in 1939. An estimated 800 desert bighorn inhabit the refuge now, but after several days we had yet to see one.

Somehow, people have managed to carve a living from this arid land for centuries. Quechan Indians farmed, fished, and hunted along the Colorado River, and they left sign of their passage, below.

Now on our way home, I had just commented that it would make our trip complete to see one.

At times, wishing can make it so. A minute later, as we topped out at the pass, I glanced up on the ridge line and spied a bighorn ram, glorious horns nearly a full three-quarter curl.

He looked down at us as if to say "I'm allowing you the privilege of looking at me."

We piled out of the truck and watched him step gingerly over the rocks, hoping he wouldn't spook before we'd gotten our fill of admiring him.

Bearing witness to these two creatures reinforces the nature of the Kofa country. The austere mountains rear up out of the desert without preface, their burnt ochre color bespeaking an explosive, fiery volcanic origin. The highest peak reaches only about 4,800 feet, and they are bereft of water, except for natural *tinajas* and artificial tanks built by hunters to lure the sheep. Their rugged, snaggle-toothed crest offers no soft edges, no invitation to saunter in sylvan glades. Access to them is formidable, save for the occasional burro or sheep trail or bushwhack up a deadend wash.

Martin Litton wrote in a 1951 issue of *Arizona Highways* that he would take an "outlander guest" to them first. "I'd give you your big dose of desert all at once. I wouldn't lead up to it gradually. I wouldn't fool around with the small fry at all. I'd take you straight to the King."

The "King" is the King of Arizona Mine, whose initials K O F A gave the mountains their name.

Fit together as neatly as a mosaic, glittering stones and pebbles armor the sands that fan out at the feet of the mountains. John C. Van Dyke, an asthmatic who sought a cure in the dry desert air, wrote that this surface is "made from tiny blocks of jasper, carnelian, agate — a pavement of pebbles so hard that a horse's hoof will make no impression upon it — wind-swept, clean, compact as though pressed down by a roller." His desert sojourns cured Van Dyke, physically and psychologically. He became the poet laureate of this landscape "of color, light and air."

Plant life grows sparsely in this land that knows a mere 5 inches of rain in a good year. A few ocotillo, creosote bushes, a saguaro cactus here and there. Yet in keeping with surprising contrasts, another plant endures here whose very presence announces "oasis." The California fan palm grows in a canyon on the west side of the Kofas. *Washingtonia filifera* is Arizona's only

Years after the Quechan chipped their messages onto the rocks, miners began to chip away at the rocks of the Chocolate Mountains, left, along the west side of the Colorado River.

native palm, and Palm Canyon and one or two others are the only places it's known in the state. A half-mile trail leads up to a view of the main grove, tucked into a moist, shaded crevice. A fire in the 1950s did a good deal of damage to the palms, but by the mid-1980s, a count totaled more than 40 individual trees. Botanists think the California palms are either leftover relics of the Ice Age or were "planted" by birds or animals that transported seeds from other locales.

When water graces the land, life flourishes in a riparian setting, right, or in a desert setting, following pages, such as the area near Dripping Springs in Organ Pipe Cactus National Monument. Here columnar cactus and Mexican poppies festoon the Puerto Blanco Mountains.

This singular country tends to attract certified colorful characters, people like old John Nummel.

A German immigrant, Nummel came to Arizona in the 1870s or early 1880s and spent the rest of his days combing these rough mountains, on foot or on the back of a burro, for flashes of gold. He worked for a while at the old Red Cloud Mine in the Trigo Mountains beside the Colorado River. But Nummel didn't get along with bosses, and one hot day he just up and walked away.

As the story goes, while pausing in the shade of a paloverde tree, he

Cholla and ocotillo, below, dot the *bajada* that fans beyond Kofa Queen Canyon. A *bajada* refers to the sloping terrain between mountains and valley floor.

The accordion pleats of saguaro cactus, right, supremely design them for life in a world of unpredictable rain. Saguaros can store tons of water in this expandable tissue to weather lean times.

hammered out a chunk of rock from a ledge — "free gold." Unlikely as it may seem, Nummel forgot about that little piece of rock as time went on; when he did try to relocate the ledge, he just couldn't find it. Nummel went to his death in 1948 without ever winning his fortune. But his lost ledge and the promise of treasure continued to draw people, including mystery author Erle Stanley Gardner, who went to the extent of looking from a helicopter. His efforts went unrewarded.

I learned about John Nummel from Smokey Knowlton, owner of Yuma River Tours out of Martinez Lake. Smokey, an evangelical river rat and part amphibious creature, makes a living running tourists up the Colorado in jet boats, hauling out stray burros, rescuing unfortunate boaters stranded

The Castle Dome
Mountains in the Kofa
National Wildlife
Refuge, above, don't
welcome humans, but
they make an ideal
home for desert
bighorn sheep. The
sheep find everything
they need here — food,
shelter, safe terrain,
and occasionally even
water.

on sandbars, and volunteering his time on projects like rebuilding the Watchman's Cabin up at the old Riverview Mine.

One December day, Smokey took us upriver to look for Nummel's place above Norton's Landing. Trying to match a 1920s photo of the site, we went ashore and scrambled through thickets of cane and tamarisk, tracing burro tracks up gullies and over hills. We tried to match the skyline with that shown in the photo, but were about to give up. As we headed back to the boat, the site presented itself, to Smokey's immense excitement.

Smokey Knowlton has his own camp now up at Norton's Landing, and one thing he'd like to do is build a replica of an old steamboat. From 1852 to 1916, steamboats were the main means of transporting ore out, and getting goods in, to mines all along the lower Colorado. Ocean schooners could navigate up the Sea of Cortés to the mouth of the Colorado, then goods were loaded onto river boats to continue upriver to Yuma and points north.

"The river steamers were to become the very lifeline of Arizona," wrote historian Richard Lingenfelter, "carrying in soldiers, miners, ranchers and merchants, and all of their rations, tools, furniture and wares; and carrying out the wealth of the mines — millions in gold, silver, copper and lead."

The boilers of the stern-wheelers were fired with uncounted cords of mesquite and cottonwood that once grew beside the river. The steamers were built with a shallow draft, and folks said a skillful captain could run

112

Teddy bear cholla, below, reproduce by shedding stems that take root when they fall to the ground.

one on a cup of water. The men who piloted the boats became legends in their own time. Capt. Isaac Polhamus, a Kentucky bachelor, was one. General manager of the Colorado Steam Navigation Company, Polhamus plied the waters from Fort Yuma upstream to Fort Mohave for nearly half a century, carrying supplies and people. One advertisement lured passengers at Yuma:

"Grand Steamer Excursion! To Stevenson's Island on the 'Mohave.' Capt. Polhamus will leave foot of Main Street at 7 A.M. Sunday, June 4, 1893, and return at 6 P.M."

Adult passage was one dollar, children 50 cents. Entertainment was music by Pablo Pino's Band.

In 1862, discoveries of gold and silver unleashed the great Colorado River Rush. A herd of prospectors and miners thundered into the Kofa country, congregating in rough-and-tumble camps and towns. On the California side, there was Tumco in the Cargo Muchacho Mountains and several diggings in the Picacho area. Other famous names were the La Paz, Fortuna, Red Cloud, Clip, numerous endeavors of Colonel Jacob Snively and Herman Ehrenberg in the Castle Dome district, the North Star, and of course the King of Arizona.

According to historian Frank Love, miners removed more than $4 million worth of gold — the best produced in Yuma County — from the King of Arizona Mine between 1897 and 1920. The vein was first discovered by Charles

For eons, the Colorado River has brought sand to the head of the Sea of Cortés. Much of this has blown back up into the Gran Desierto and Algodones Dunes south and west of Yuma. The wind constantly reshapes the surface of these dunes in ever-changing patterns, below and right.

Life in the desert calls for a quick response to even the lightest shower. Ocotillo, following pages, a relative of the boojum tree of Baja California, can sprout leaves several times a year after rains fall around Kofa Queen Canyon.

Eichelberger, who much like John Nummel was said to have been resting in the shade of a tree one day when he noticed bright yellow spots on a rock overhang. After staking his claim and settling the question of his rightful shares, Eichelberger soon sold his interests to Eugene Ives, a Tucson lawyer and politician. It wasn't long before disputes kept the owners in and out of court, arguing over who was defrauding whom of profits.

One high roller, Felix Mayhew, reportedly lit his cigars with 20-dollar bills after he sold out his interest in the North Star Mine.

Mining was low-tech in the early days: rawhide ore buckets, candles wired to miner's hats, and payment in token or scrip, accepted only at company stores and saloons. Camp housing was in such short supply that men were charged to sleep on the ground. Many miners ended up building their own homes, like "Brass Band" Bill Smith's simple stick-and-mud house at the Kofa. At its peak, some 750 people called the Kofa home, while Castle Dome City, located in the neighboring mountains, had as many people as Yuma did.

In 1899, with a source of permanent water and temporary resolution of lawsuits, the Kofa was going full blast. An elementary school for 16 students

was to open the following year. And, the same report noted, the general manager "hires mostly Cornish miners from Cornwall, England. They have brought their families with them, so Kofa tends to be a quieter mining town than usual."

By 1907, the King of Arizona Mine was on a downhill slide. The ore played out, and the mine shut down for good in 1910. Today, the remains of the Kofa and neighboring North Star and Polaris mines are accessible in the south end of the range — mostly crumbling buildings; tailings piles; mounds of broken crockery, blue glass, and rusted tin cans; and signs on private property warning "Stay on Designated Roads" and "Danger Cyanide."

The sound of the wind rules the place.

The center of civilization — for miners, steamboat captains, freighters, railroaders, soldiers, entrepreneurs, Spaniards, and Indians alike — was the place just below the confluence of the Gila River with the Colorado, known as Yuma Crossing. Here the Colorado could be forded. Local Quechan Indians had been using the crossing for a long time before any Euro-Americans came on the scene.

The Quechan believe their spiritual leader Kumastamxo taught them to hunt, fish, and farm. They settled along the river in *rancherías*, growing cotton, tobacco, corn, melons, and beans. They were strong warriors, who made war clubs of hard mesquite, bows of willow, and arrows of cane. Tall and robust, they were also remarkable runners and swimmers. Dreams were the source of their power, and their stories are still told in song.

Early Spanish explorers followed the Gila River down to the Colorado. In 1700, Father Eusebio Kino, with the Indians' help, crossed the Colorado in a basket mounted on a raft. Juan Bautista de Anza likewise benefited from their assistance on his way to California. While these encounters were friendly, the arrival of Fray Tómas Garcés turned disastrous. In 1779, Garcés convinced the Spanish authorities to establish a mission at Yuma. Settlers soon followed and built villages along the river. The Indians' initial friendliness turned to hostility as the Spaniards began irrigating and putting their animals out to graze on the best farm and pasture lands. The Quechan secretly planned a revolt, and in a surprise attack on the morning of July 17, 1781, they killed more than 100 Spaniards, including Garcés.

The Quechan controlled the strategic crossing into the 1800s — until

A *bajada* at the foot of Signal Peak in the Kofa Mountains, below, provides a transition between craggy uplifts and relatively flat land.

soldiers arrived during the United States' war with Mexico. In 1847, Philip St. George Cooke and his Mormon Battalion came down the Gila and crossed the Colorado near Yuma. At the end of the war, forty-niners flowed through this natural funnel, ferried across the river by the Quechan and the soldiers. Various attempts to seize the ferry operations from the Quechan failed, until 1852. In that year, Maj. Samuel P. Heintzelman occupied the crossing and set up Fort Yuma on the California side of the river.

Colorado City (later Arizona City, then Yuma) was established by Charles D. Poston and Herman Ehrenberg in 1854. The first business to open its doors in Arizona City was Sarah Bowman's restaurant. A brawny 6-footer, Bowman earned her nickname "The Great Western" with her resemblance to a steamboat. Though she chose to stay, she characterized Yuma territory as "a thin tissue of sand over the fires of hell."

122

Stagecoaches soon were ferrying across the Colorado River at Yuma. In 1858, *New York Herald* correspondent Waterman Ormsby described the experience:

"The boat is a sort of flatboat, and is propelled by the rapid current, being kept in its course by pulleys running on a rope stretched across the river. We crossed just at daybreak and found the few Americans ready to receive us. After a hasty breakfast we changed our horses and were off again."

Yuma's summer heat seared into the minds of many who visited. Another reporter for an eastern newspaper wrote, "This is the hottest place in the world; so hot in the summertime that the wings melt off the mosquitoes."

Yet Yuma persisted as a key link in movement across the formidable desert. By 1877, the Southern Pacific Railroad bridged the Colorado and charged across Arizona. Railroads put the steamboats out of business, but in not too many years, the automobile would supersede the railroads. By the early teens, automobiles traveled on the southern Ocean-to-Ocean Highway, and in 1915, a brand-spanking-new steel highway bridge was completed across the Colorado at Yuma.

Yet an obstacle remained. Just west of Yuma loomed California's Algodones Dunes, which had stymied travelers even before the time of the Model T. In 1915, wooden planks laid for 10 miles through the dunes made a portable road that could be picked up and relocated as the sands blew over it.

The lower Colorado's seasonal flooding rampages created additional problems for Yuma. In 1909, Laguna Dam was built upstream, launching the federal government's era of "reclamation" of the desert. It was the first of a series of dams — Imperial Dam and Hoover Dam came next in the 1930s — along with canals and channels that rendered the Colorado a tamed being, at least temporarily. The tinkerings stanched flows and allowed irrigation of thousands of acres of lettuce, broccoli, and citrus, surreal green rectangles amid the desert terrain. Yuma kicks up its heels each January with Lettuce Days — the *pièce de résistance* is the world's biggest tossed salad.

The Colorado is tamed and easily crossed these days. But birds still flock to it, and you can almost smell the water, even in the dry mountains to the east. Terns and bighorn sheep bear witness that some wildness remains in this land. ॐ

An ocotillo decorates a *bajada* at Kofa Queen Canyon, above.

123

Hualapai Mountains

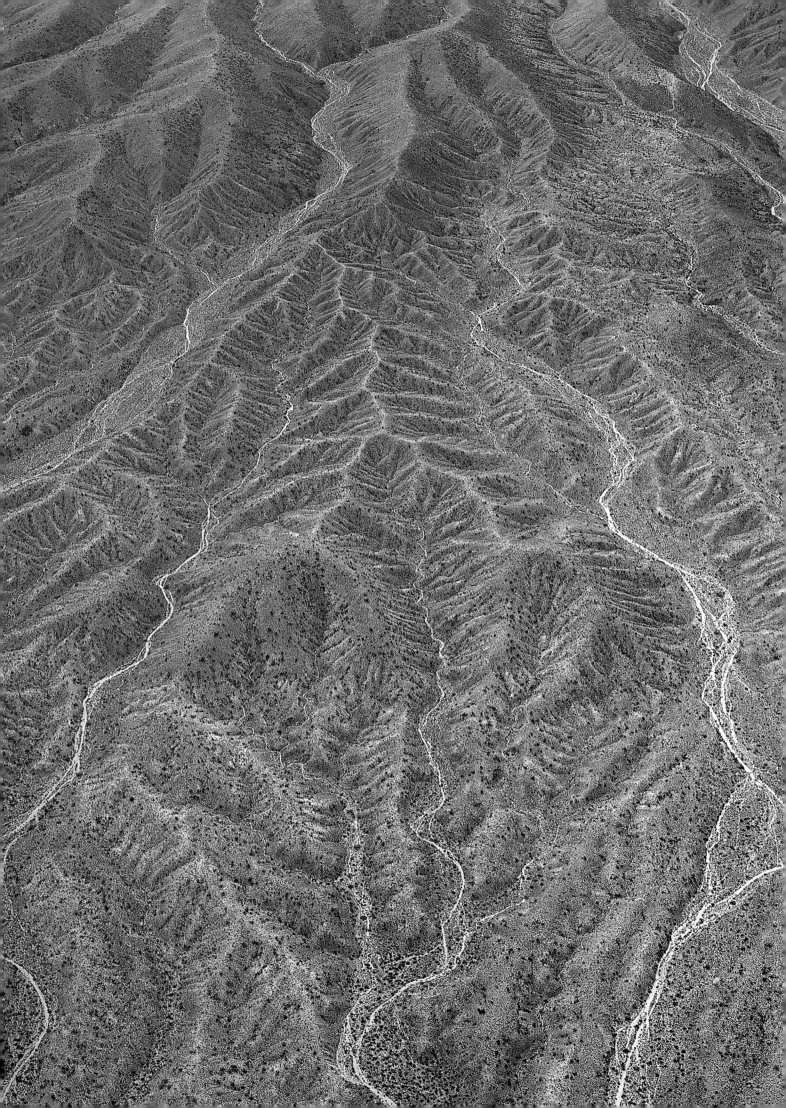

Hualapai Mountains

Deserts Converge Here

I f a person wanted to go somewhere in Arizona and not see a soul for 40 days and 40 nights, the upper reaches of Burro Creek could be the place. At least that's what Bob Hall, public affairs officer for the Bureau of Land Management (BLM) in Kingman, suggested to an acquaintance who wanted to mark his 40th year in this way.

The man followed Hall's suggestion, put on his backpack, and started walking. But it was winter, and the sun doesn't warm the banks of upper Burro Creek much. Still, the man sustained his dream for 30 of the 40 days, and he never did encounter another human being.

The wilds of Burro Creek are only a small part of about 5 million acres of public land in northwestern Arizona, from the Grand Wash Cliffs at the western end of Grand Canyon, south to Alamo Lake on the Bill Williams River, and west to Topock on the lower Colorado River. The region includes the Black, Cerbat, and Music mountains in the north; and the Rawhide, Poachie, Arrastra, and McCracken ranges in the south and southwest.

In the center of this region rise the Hualapai Mountains.

Elevation ranges from 600 feet above sea level at Topock to 8,417 feet on

Western Arizona is wild land. If a person wanted to forsake the world for a time, this would be the place to go, especially somewhere like the Mount Nutt Wilderness in the Black Mountains northwest of the Hualapais, preceding pages. Water that eventually flows into the Big Sandy River first carves dendritic patterns on the east side of the Hualapai Mountains, left.

Rising to 8,417 feet, the
summits of the
Hualapai Mountains,
below, attract clouds
and lightning which
ignites fires in the
ponderosa forest that
clings to this range.

Hualapai Peak — from low desert, to foothills, to forested highlands. Such a vast difference means precipitation varying from 6 inches to as much as 24 inches a year. And it means lots of places for animals to live.

If you called Bob Hall a bit "batty," he'd take the remark as a compliment. His office is decorated with bat posters, bat drawings, bat houses, and other bat-related paraphernalia. This former BLM wildlife biologist, before transferring to public affairs, had been monitoring these flying mammals at one mine for more than a decade, and he continues to be a loyal friend of these often much-maligned creatures. With thousands of abandoned mines available to bats for day and night roosts and hibernation and maternity colonies, the Hualapai region harbors an amazing array of bat species. Using mist nets, night vision equipment, and specialized computers that analyze bats' sonar signals, other researchers have documented 19 species, including four not previously known in the area.

In addition to bats, the Hualapais are the only place where another rare little mammal is found. This one doesn't fly. Instead, it spends most of its life out of sight under the ground. It's the Hualapai Mexican vole, first found in 1923 by mammalogist E.A. Goldman.

He collected four of them near the top of Hualapai Peak and described this new animal for science. Further attempts to find the voles through the 1980s turned up only 15 individuals. These mouse-sized voles have a short tail and short legs; long, loose, cinnamon-brown fur; and a diagnostic blunt nose. And though the voles themselves are not often seen, their presence shows in the form of burrow entrances, fecal pellets, and caches of cut greenery in miniature "runways" connecting their burrows.

The green grass the voles eat is thought to stimulate their breeding cycle. Hualapai Mexican voles prefer grassy places among the scattered pockets of ponderosa pine, often near seeps and springs, the same places where elk, cattle, and campers also like to congregate. The vole is listed as an endangered species and was possibly on the brink of extinction in the mid-1980s when only one desk-top-sized piece of habitat was known. The species still survives, though, thanks to protection of its habitat and cooperation among private landowners, ranchers, and government agencies.

The plant life of the Hualapai country is extraordinary. A partial list shows creosote bush, saguaro cactus, paloverde, Joshua tree forests, chaparral of

Dean Peak, in the
foreground at left,
wears a wreath of
clouds.

The outlandish Joshua tree, below, is the trademark of the Mojave Desert. Elders with thick gray, cork-like bark can reach 200 years in age.

Among the best examples of Joshuas are those in the valleys around the Hualapai Mountains, right.

oak, manzanita, silk tassel, sugar sumac, single-leaf piñon, bear grass, buck-thorn, Mormon tea, desert honeysuckle, cliffrose, mountain mahogany, buck-wheat, twinberry, hackberry, Apache plume, hoptree, elderberry, black cherry, wild raspberry, along with junipers and ponderosa pine. The Hualapai range is the only one for a hundred miles in any direction that is high enough to support a forest community of Douglas fir, white fir, and even aspen in the uppermost reaches.

Down in the desert foothills that roll out at the base of the mountains, plant life can be extravagant like it was in the spring of 1884, a bountiful wildflower year. There that May to see it, geologist and botanist Marcus Jones exclaimed, the desert "was a perfect garden in all directions, never was as good for 20 years afterwards."

One of his prize specimens was a plant called the white-margined

Wild tobacco, below left, frequents washes and sandy bottoms, while evening primrose, below right, grows on slopes and plains.

penstemon that he found near Yucca, Arizona. Jones described the penstemon, with lavender-pink flowers and distinctive white-edged leaves, as "a most conspicuous and remarkable plant." Jones was fortunate to see it, because for most of the year this penstemon is normally not even visible. To survive the dryness, the plant's leaves die back to the ground; it emerges and blooms only in those springtimes that are preceded by generous and well-timed winter rains. Arizona's one and only population of this rare plant grows in a limited area of sandy washes and ridges on the west side of the Huala-pais. (Only three widely separated populations of this plant are known in three states, and the Hualapai group has the largest number of individual plants.) Through a historic land exchange completed in 1999, according to Bob Hall, BLM resolved a difficult intermingled land ownership situation and consolidated a good portion of the plant's Mojave Desert habitat into a solid, manageable piece of public land. The home of the white-margined penstemon will be protected from surrounding development within an ACEC — Area of Critical Environmental Concern.

In certain places in and around the Hualapais, there exists an astounding juxtaposition of two major North American deserts — the Sonoran and Mojave. That happy situation shows up when the Sonoran Desert's signature

The Mojave and Sonoran deserts overlap in the Hualapai Mountain country. In spring, owl clover, globemallow, and lupine, left, enliven the walk into Kaiser Spring. Young saguaro cactus, following pages, have the best shot at becoming old saguaro cactus if they happen to germinate beneath the shelter of a paloverde tree, or other "nurse" plant, as did this saguaro in the Aubrey Hills south of the Hualapais.

The creamy-white flowers of Joshua trees, below, form clusters on the tips of the spiked branches and require a particular moth for their pollination.

saguaro cactus grows within the arms of the Mojave Desert's trademark Joshua tree. Here too, the venerable desert tortoise finds high-quality habitat. Another ACEC, of more than 20,000 acres, has been established in the granite-strewn McCracken Mountains, southwest of the Hualapais. This is essential for the survival of the tortoises, along with companion species including the rosy boa, chuckwalla, and Gila monster.

Three rivers course through this amazing desert country — the Big Sandy, the Santa Maria, and the Bill Williams. Knight and Trout creeks join above the little roadside town of Wikieup to form the Big Sandy. The river lazes down through the valley on the east side of the Hualapais; after Burro Creek joins in, the Big Sandy meets the Santa Maria to form the Bill Williams at the south end of the range. That confluence now is under the waters of Alamo Lake.

Flanked on both sides by wide valleys, the Hualapais run north to south for 40 miles. Geologist Ivo Lucchitta characterizes them as "classic Nevada-style" Basin and Range mountains. In fact, the Hualapais and the Big Sandy Valley are at the edge between the Basin and Range geologic province to the north and west and the canyon and mesa country of the Colorado Plateau to the east.

We went camping one weekend with Ivo and his wife, Baerbel, also a geologist, out into the desert south of the Hualapais. Ivo knows this country like the back of his hand, or perhaps more accurately the bottom of his feet. To him, the Hualapais are a fairly well-behaved mountain range compared to the ragged country to the southwest. The only real way to unravel the geology is to set out on foot and look up close at the rocks. That's what Ivo did, over many winters.

On our weekend together, we headed to one of his favorite spots, Centennial Wash, which drains south into the Bill Williams River. After following the Lucchittas' fishtailing VW van down the wash's soft sandy bed, we got out and walked an old jeep road to a tributary of Centennial. Ivo informally named it Thanksgiving Wash, since he and a colleague gave thanks when they finally figured out the story of the rocks. Another nearby area so perplexed them for a while that they called it Confusion Basin.

Stopping at a large gray streamside boulder, we spread out the geologic map, splotched with pinks, greens, blues, and yellows denoting basalts, rhyolites, breccias, and alluvium. All of this is part of a region of "highly extended

Members of the yucca family, Joshua trees form entire forests. Their favored habitat lies in the mid-elevations of the desert mountains — like the stand, left, along the Chicken Springs Road that crosses the Hualapais.

terrain," ragged low mountains broken like slivers of tilted china plates, formed by a stupendous stretching of the earth's crust.

Like Lucchitta, though, folks know that summer is not the best time to be out here. People from the desert towns of Bullhead and Lake Havasu City flee the sizzling heat and seek refuge in the Hualapais' cool heights. If they come too early in the season, or stay too late, they can get a rude surprise. When we stopped to inquire about camping in Hualapai Mountain Park, the ranger advised us not to get stuck in the snow like some guys did recently — "Grown men," she said in a can-you-believe-it voice. As we departed, she wished us well and told us to carry plenty of water.

In what is now the park, a few hardy settlers once grew potatoes up at 7,000 feet. An old photograph shows three men by a log cabin, where reportedly "good potato crops were grown." The cabin belonged to W.H. Shoulters, who discovered the nearby American Flag Mine. On a brisk November morning, we hike the namesake Potato Patch Loop trail. It switchbacks up past gorgeous old yellow-belly ponderosa pines and impressive white firs. Browned leaves rattle in copses of Gambel oaks. Pumpkin-colored lichens plaster the

The Black Mountains, above, stand guard on the Arizona side of the Colorado River. Volcanic in origin, they form part of the great Basin and Range Province that stretches northward into Nevada and Utah.

big gray boulders. The highest peaks — Aspen, Hayden, and Hualapai — are granite spires of gold and pink and tan. When the trail swings into a bowl on their north side, it feels more like a place to grow icicles than potatoes. No time to linger — the first real winter storm is blowing in from California, and the ranger's tale of the men stuck in snow echoes in our minds.

The Hualapai Mountains carry the name of the Hualapai Indians — the "People of the Ponderosa" or "Pine People." Their homeland included about 5 million acres in northwestern Arizona. In their oral history, Judaba:h (Younger Earth-Brother) told them:

> You Hualapai, you Hualapai, / This is what your name is going to be. / Nowhere, no far away lands, / Different lands, some strange lands belonging to others, / You are not to go or be anywhere. / Here, the water that lies here, / The land here, the land along this river, / Here, you roam here, / Be around here, / You are to be here, it is destined. / Things, / The fish, the water, / Springs flow, it is so. / That water, that wood, whatever you are to eat is prepared. / They are around here.

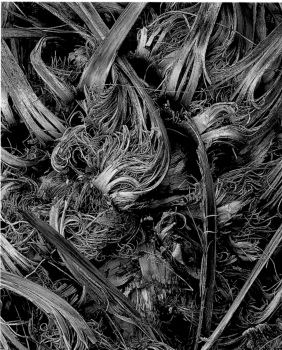

A decomposing yucca, below, reveals the fibers that were so useful to Indians.

The Hualapai were familiar with every inch of their land. They followed plants and animals through the seasons. In the spring, they harvested and roasted stalks of yucca. The seeds of stickleaf and fruits of cactus were good in summer. In certain autumns, they collected fat piñon nuts and stored them for winter. They irrigated gardens with waters from the streams and springs. Using a barbed wooden stick, they pulled puffed-out chuckwallas from rock crevices. They also ate woodrats and hunted mule deer, bighorn sheep, and pronghorn antelope. The Hualapai were part of a trade network with neighboring tribes, bartering their specialties of dried mescal, red hematite, and exquisitely made seed-gathering and burden baskets.

The Hualapai managed to remain fairly intact until the 1850s, when government explorers and surveyors made incursions into their territory. Lorenzo Sitgreaves, A.W. Whipple, and Edward Beale came through looking for transcontinental railroad routes. Fort Mohave was established on the Colorado River, and gold was discovered. Hostilities escalated, and raids and battles occurred on both sides. Chief Wauba Yuma was killed in 1866, setting off the "Hualapai War," in which his son, Quasula, was a major leader.

Along the Potato Patch
Trail, a veneer of lichen
dapples a rock face,
below.

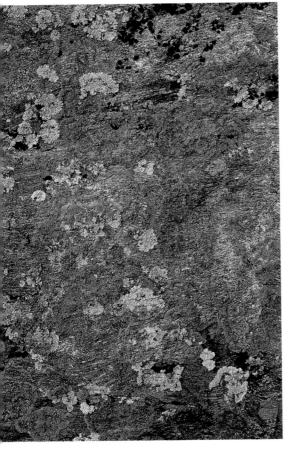

In December 1868, U.S. Army Maj. William Redwood Price took 25 men and went south along the Hualapai Mountains, staying high, according to Major Price, "up near the snowy peak, traveling over the roughest trail I ever moved on."

Discovering a large Hualapai *rancheria*, Price and his troops moved in and killed eight Indians and took 14 women and children captive. He reported that the *rancheria* had "one horse, 50 buckskins, 12 bows and over 100 arrows, 1 pistol, powder and bullets, 1 axe, 200 buckets, containing provisions, 25 pairs of moccasins, 3 saddles, 12 water jugs, [a] number of bags containing seeds, corn, piñon nuts, with several hundred pounds of prepared muscal [sic], together with the most completed lot of minor articles, very valuable to them, that I have ever seen in an Indian camp."

The war ended in 1869. Over the next several years, the Hualapai were held at Camp Beale Springs just outside Kingman, and then at La Paz on the lower Colorado. In 1876, Gen. George Crook wrote that "their condition is deplorable; being mountain Indians, the heat of the place with a want of proper diet has produced an eruptive disease, which seems to have become epidemic. Many of their small children are nearly blind, the result of the glare of the sun and drifting sand."

By 1882, when the Hualapai returned to their original territory, Anglos had moved in and taken over their land. A year later, they were given a reservation that consisted of about a tenth of their original homeland. The Hualapai participated in the messianic Ghost Dance that gave temporary hope to Indians in the West, but the last dance was held in 1895.

A wagon road passed across the foothills of the Hualapai Mountains, part of the Mohave-Prescott Toll Road that ran 160 miles from Fort Mohave to Prescott. It was the first "public highway" in Mohave County, approved by the Territorial Legislature in 1864. Tolls were set at 1 cent a mile for a wagon drawn by two horses; 3/4 of a cent for a carriage or cart drawn by one horse; and one-half cent per mile for each pack animal. Travelers stopped for water at various springs — Beale's, Hualapai, Cottonwood, and Free's.

Martha Summerhayes, wife of Army man Jack Summerhayes, made the journey on the road across the Mojave Desert in 1874. Her impressions at the time were less than complimentary. At Beale's Spring just outside present-day Kingman, the ranch resembled other way stations she had encountered,

Gambel oaks, right,
sprout at the base of a
cliff composed of
granite, the backbone
of the Hualapai
Mountains. The
Hualapais look west to
the Colorado River as it
flows through Topock
Gorge, following pages.

A ground cover, below, grows in the area of Lake Mead, at the upper end of Hualapai country .

"except that possibly it was even more desolate." Nonetheless, it had one redeeming feature. "A German lived there, who must have had some knowledge of cooking, for I remember that we bought a peach pie from him and ate it with a relish," Martha added.

But hindsight tempered those initial negative reactions to the landscape. In her famed memoir *Vanished Arizona,* written years after her Arizona sojourn, Martha Summerhayes recalled, "I did not see much to admire in the desolate waste lands through which we were travelling. I did not dream of the power of the desert, nor that I should ever long to see it again. But as I write, the longing possesses me . . . to come back."

Prospectors came into the Hualapais and surrounding mountains in search of valuable minerals. By the late 1870s, more than 100 mines were located in the Hualapais. Gold, silver, copper, zinc, tungsten, molybdenum, and tellurium have all been mined here at one time or another. Greenwood

From less than 4,000 feet to mid-5,000-foot levels, the Black Mountains, left, stand lower than the Hualapais and closer to the Colorado River.

Deep red claretcup
cactus, below, stands
out in the Cerbat
Mountains near the
town of Chloride.

Claretcups bloom with
gusto, right, in the
warm, sunny climate.

City, located not far from where Burro Creek empties into the Big Sandy, was thriving. There, *The Miner* newspaper reported on June 22, 1877, the "Davis House is well patronized, offers the traveler clean beds and a luxurious table. Heavy stocks of goods are carried by Solomon & Myers, Kimble Brothers and Levy & Koshland. Money is plentiful, business is on a cash basis. A good physician is there. There are no lawyers there, the people are law-abiding."

Alas, Greenwood didn't last. Its place was taken by the burg of Signal, mill town for the McCracken mines. But by 1886, the boom had gone bust there also.

We took the Signal Road one April day as the desert was putting on a stupendous once-in-a-decade-or-two floral show. Heading west, we forded the Big Sandy at shallow places a couple of times. We backtracked to camp for the night in a spot agog with wildflowers. Near sunset, I sat on a boulder amid

A barrel cactus, below, sidles up to a brittlebush plant in the Black Mountains north of Union Pass.

A barrel cactus, below, sidles up to a brittlebush plant in the Black Mountains north of Union Pass.

brittlebush, lupine, buckwheat, tackstem, and a plant I'd never seen before, a pale delphinium. Back in the camper, birds kept me awake a good part of the night. It was breeding season, and they must have been working 'round the clock. I could have sworn some were saying "come here, come here, come here."

The next morning, the warm honey calls of doves played soothing background music. I walked along the old road on a quest for the perfect mariposa lily — delicate lilac petals atop frail stems, the inner sanctum of the flower marked with deep purple spots. This, one of nature's most exquisite creations, is only one of many riches secreted in the Hualapai Mountain country. ∽

Cholla, left, inviting to look at but wicked to touch, grows along the Santa Maria River.

Navajo Mountain

Navajo | Mountain

*Centerpiece
of the
Colorado Plateau*

T he van's wheels spun in the sand and stopped. We piled out, stashed water bottles, cinched up straps on our packs, eased the loads onto our backs, and started walking. Past a Navajo hogan and a sheep pen with a scarecrow, we saw the monumental stack of rocks, the cairn marking the head of the trail around the north side of Navajo Mountain.

It was a clear April Monday with a cool breeze. Perfect hiking weather. For the next 5 days, we would be in the constant presence of this imposing mountain the Navajo call Naatsis'aan, "Pollen Mountain," the head of a reclining female.

The blue dome of Navajo Mountain floats on the horizon, visible from nearly 100 miles away. "It is quite solitary, without even a foothill for society, and its very loneliness is impressive," wrote geologist Clarence Dutton.

Rising to 10,388 feet above sea level, and forested with ponderosa pine, spruce, fir, and aspen, Navajo Mountain straddles the Arizona-Utah border. On talus slopes near the top, groundwater surfaces as War God Spring and others, where locals make pilgrimages to get "sweet water."

We were 11 souls, on an *Arizona Highways* photography workshop led by

Sandstone country surrounds Navajo Mountain, a land of spires, buttes, mesas, and domes. The monoliths of Monument Valley, preceding pages, stand guard over mysterious country in Navajoland. Erosion shaped the rocks of Cummings Mesa, left, on the west side of Navajo Mountain, into fantastic fins, arches, slots, and natural bridges.

The defining rock of this place is named Navajo sandstone — a wind-blown amalgam of nearly pure quartz sand piled thousands of feet high. The sandstone erodes easily under even the smallest desert stream, leaving a maze of intricate swirls as seen on Gray Mesa on Kaibito Plateau, below.

Michael Collier. I got to tag along as guest scribe and amateur botanist. We convened in Page, then drove south past Inscription House and in on a dirt road for miles. After passing the small community of Rainbow City, where front yards contain horses and satellite dishes, the road ends in sand and the trail begins.

Darla and Bud, the two "bookends" in age, struck up an immediate friendship. Bud was an experienced mountaineer; Darla, a willing student. For the rest of the trip, she practiced the useful rock climbing knots he demonstrated.

The first day out, we hiked only about 3 miles, to Cha, "Beaver," Canyon. Water ran in the creek bed, and a convention of canyon tree frogs bleated like hoarse sheep, such small creatures to make such a huge racket. After pitching camp, we explored down-canyon and found a pair of old hogans of logs and dirt, blending seamlessly into the surroundings. The hogans had been abandoned for some time, but we weren't sure of their age. They could have been built as early as the 1860s and occupied as late as the 1940s.

In 1866, Hashke'niinii, or Hoskanini, led a group of Navajo families into the impenetrable fastness of sandstone canyons that swirls at the base of Navajo Mountain. They were hiding from Kit Carson and his U.S. Army troops, who were on a full-scale campaign to rout all the Navajos from their homeland and force them to a holding area on the Pecos River in New Mexico. Navajo tradition holds that the gods helped Hashke'niinii by sending floods down the San Juan River that stopped Carson and his men.

Each August, on Navajo Mountain Pioneer Day, people gather to honor those elders who escaped the horrors of the Long Walk, as the Navajos call the sad journey to New Mexico. Grandmothers and grandfathers, dressed in their best velvet shirts and turquoise jewelry, solemnly carry out the Little Long Walk. They proceed down the length of the dusty parade ground and in front of the reviewing stand bow their heads and pray in Navajo. Translated: "This is in remembrance of our old ways, our grandparents, this is in their memory . . . now we go back to remember how they used to live."

That first night in Cha Canyon, the cool breath of Navajo Mountain drove the temperature down into the 30s. We huddled around the juniper fire, eating simple dinners before cocooning into the warmth of our sleeping bags. In the morning, the trail wove through the rock wonderland toward Nasja Canyon. Nurtured by ample moisture, spring wildflowers everywhere splashed

With patterned, perpendicular cliffs, Oak Canyon, left, demonstrates how Navajo sandstone dominates the area.

157

The broad-shouldered dome of Navajo Mountain, below, looms for a hundred miles in every direction. The mountain formed when an uplifting fist of magma bowed up the surrounding strata but failed to break through to the surface.

A golden streamer of cottonwoods, right, spills down Aztec Creek on the southwestern side of Navajo Mountain.

the ground with color — pink penstemon, white sego lily, indigo larkspur, yellow evening primrose — along with battalions of caterpillars crawling through the black brush.

Scrambling on top of high knobs, we were moved to silence by the endless view into southern Utah — the Kaiparowits Plateau, the Henry Mountains, the Waterpocket Fold, the Circle Cliffs — infinite as the ocean. We came back down and descended a steep hillside into Bald Rock Canyon, home to another luxurious flowing stream. Over lunch, we talked geology, prompted by our entry into the domain of Navajo sandstone.

Navajo Mountain is the centerpiece of the Colorado Plateau, and the Navajo sandstone makes up its pure heart.

Geologist Herbert Gregory, Michigan born and Yale educated, roamed this country in the early 20th century. In 1947, an editor had this to say about

A block of Wingate sandstone in Nokai Canyon, below, accents Chinle shale, formed from the sediment of waters that dried up ages ago.

Dr. Gregory: "[He] has been coming to this region nearly every year since 1900 . . . trying to piece together the story of the ancient past."

From his investigations, Gregory published thorough reports and beautiful maps that are classics. He liked the country pretty well: "The region is seen to possess a ruggedness probably surpassed by few other parts of the world. . . . The intricacy and grandeur of the stream-carved sculpture are unexcelled in any other part of the Plateau province."

It was Gregory who in 1915 named the Navajo sandstone — rock that "is everywhere a cliff maker," he wrote. "The explorer soon learns that the way by which he entered a canyon may be the only mode of exit."

Navajo sandstone dates to Jurassic times — the days of the dinosaurs — 190 to 170 million years ago. Jurassic winds piled grain upon grain of nearly pure quartz sand into sheets of dunes stretching from what is now central Wyoming to southern Nevada, cemented into a rock layer that masses more than 1,000 feet high around Navajo Mountain and more than double that in places such as Zion National Park in Utah. Sweeping curves of crossbeds memorialize the ancient wind currents on the face of the Navajo. Its colors are variously creamy white, tan, buff, yellow, and orange. The Navajo fractures

Nature paints this country with an exotic brush, resulting in the varnished cliff wall of Navajo sandstone, left, in Secret Canyon.

At Navajo Mountain, below, sandstone knobs rise above Oak Bay on Lake Powell.

Cottonwoods, right, seek water tumbling from a spring flowing into Piute Canyon. Groundsel, following pages, grows on sand dunes near Shonto Trading Post, southeast of Navajo Mountain.

like a big conch shell and weathers into arches, fins, rounded knolls, and vertical-walled canyons so slender that, with arms outstretched, a person can touch both sides. It forms alcoves with 180-degree arcs overhead, the closest things to cathedrals that nature constructs.

This fantastic accumulation of rock was buried underground for another 100 million years, until the first uplift of the Colorado Plateau, which coincided with the raising of the Rocky Mountains about 60 to 70 million years ago. Navajo Mountain punched into the plateau between 25 to 39 million years ago. The mountain is a laccolith, a word meaning "stone cistern," formed when a well of magma, or molten rock, intruded from deep underground, pooling and spreading beneath the surface and doming up the overlying sedimentary layers. The Colorado Plateau is heaven for laccolith lovers. Several other isolated examples dot the neighborhood — the Carrizos in Arizona; the Henrys, Abajos, and La Sals in Utah; and Ute Mountain in southwestern Colorado — all

162

An alcove in Water Holes Canyon, below, overlooks a clutch of redbud and cottonwood trees, hardy survivors in this arid land.

apparently formed at about the same time as Navajo Mountain.

The plateau saw another period of radical uprising about 17 million years ago, lifting the entire province more than a mile above sea level and raising the laccolithic bubbles right along with it. The scene was set for melting snows off Navajo Mountain and sudden, powerful summer flash floods to begin etching canyons into raw rock, like a lithographer practicing his art. Stone turned to sand, to be turned to stone again.

The pull out of Bald Rock Canyon the next morning, over little more than a sketch of a trail, was a workout. Bald Rock is one of the deep, sinuous canyons weaving a maze around Navajo Mountain. They can be crossed only at a few of their shallower places. At a low pass, our efforts were rewarded with more inspiring views northward. We knew that the space between us and the far distance was filled with the mirror glint of Lake Powell. The lake wasn't visible to us, however, and we could dream that the exquisite place known as

A tumbleweed, left, is a passing visitor to Fall Canyon.

167

This country, so often only bare rock, can harbor delicacy in the bloom of a sacred datura, below left, and the plumed seed head of a cliffrose, below right.

Glen Canyon was not submerged, that "progress" had not intruded into this last remnant of sheer wild land.

In contrast to our first chilly night, the afternoon sun bordered on hot. When we reached Nasja Canyon and Surprise Valley, a picnic table awaited. The photographers headed out to see what there was to see. Back in camp, it was too windy for a fire, so it was early to bed. Substantial clouds gathered around the head of Navajo Mountain during the night, and in a sleepy stupor, we decided against pitching our tarp; for once, we guessed right.

Wednesday: clear sky. After a quick breakfast of coffee and oatmeal, we took a short side trip up to a small ancient granary tucked under an alcove. Several people managed the steep climb up to it. Jim, from the flat forests of Minnesota, caught on quickly to the art of standing up straight, trusting his feet on the tilted rock face. David, a botanist from Australia, reported a "picture-window view." Bud scrambled up and found a deceased porcupine nearby and a piñon tree with signs where the animal had fed. Another detour led to a small stone arch named Owl Bridge. We continued to see signs of Navajo habitation — a small structure of juniper logs, a sweat lodge most likely, and another old hogan.

Oak Creek, the next major drainage curving down off Navajo Mountain, beckoned with big cottonwood trees and abundant water. Following a steep, boulder-strewn path, we dropped into the creek bed and were impressed by

Water Holes Canyon, right, is a vertical world of glowing slickrock and swirling shadows.

168

the diligent beavers that had gnawed down sizable cottonwoods. From our streamside camp, we made a foray "just around a bend" downstream to see a cave. A fascinating place: handprints and a human figure painted on the back wall and deposits that we surmised had piled up since the last ice age. In similar deposits nearby, paleontologists have found bones and dung from big mammals like ground sloths and mammoths that trundled through this canyon country some 12,000 years ago. We trundled back to camp, but found pools along the way that were too good to pass up; Peter, an uninhibited Belgian, led the way in for a swim.

A half-moon alcove, below, perfectly frames a redbud tree in Bridge Canyon, one of many surprises that delight hikers trekking around the north side of Navajo Mountain.

Thursday: up and out of Oak Creek, then a hard right into Bridge Canyon. Lunch was beside a delightful basin of water known locally as the "Maiden's Pool." Everyone was down to the last of their food stashes, and bartering was fast and furious. Kris gave away her peanut butter, but Mark failed to entice anyone with the dregs of his trail mix. The sun emerged, making for a toasty walk down to the confluence where Redbud Canyon joins Bridge Canyon. The group voted to spend the last 2 nights under a roomy overhang in Bridge Canyon, a niche strewn with a miniature rainforest of Virginia creeper and a hanging garden of columbine and maidenhair fern. At night, we gazed at the lens of black sky and made wishes on the promises of shooting stars.

From this base camp, we poked back up Bridge and Redbud canyons, laboring up the tight, 700-foot incline of Redbud Pass and over into Cliff Canyon, where the trail leads out to the other side of Navajo Mountain.

Friday: a long one for some. Ten miles down and back to Forbidding

Rainbow Bridge, above, the world's highest natural bridge, spans the walls of Bridge Canyon.

171

Water is wealth in this slickrock country. Life long ago learned to thrive in its presence. Bridge Creek, below, nourishes a pocket of redbud trees, which bloom with exquisite pink flowers in spring.

Pools along Bridge Canyon, right, permit ephemeral creatures like canyon tree frogs to complete their life cycles.

Canyon. Notorious "Collier Miles," as group wisdom came to call them. Jay and Susan could not resist the temptation, and they opted for a reconnaissance trip down Bridge Canyon to catch a glimpse of Rainbow Bridge. Unlike an arch, weathered out over dry land by wind and chemical means, a natural bridge starts from the erosion of a flowing stream beneath it. Given a few hundred thousand years, the water running in Bridge Canyon delivered enough erosive material — boulders and pebbles and sand — to abandon a meander and gnaw a shortcut through a fin of sandstone. *Voilà*, Rainbow Bridge. Rising 290 feet above the streambed, with a span of 275 feet, it is the largest natural bridge in the world.

Saturday: The last day of the trip came much too soon. We walked the last few leisurely miles down to Rainbow Bridge, stopping at Echo Camp (complete with old bedsprings). We lunched under another alcove, where we found an inscription scratched into the rock:

172

Entrada sandstone
boulders, below, line
the bottom of Potato
Canyon on White Mesa.

John Wetherill

8/14/1909

This was the signature of the Oljeto, Utah, trader who was among the group of Anglos who "discovered" the now-famous natural bridge, Nonnezoshe, "Rainbow-turned-to-stone."

Although Indians knew of it for perhaps a thousand years or more, their obvious claim is unrecorded in writing. Dispute remains over who among whites saw Rainbow Bridge first. Prospectors left their names nearby in the 1880s; some said government surveyor W.B. Douglass earned the honor; Neil Judd insisted it was his uncle, Byron Cummings, dean at the University of Utah; while author Zane Grey credited John Wetherill, who led him into Rainbow Bridge in 1913.

Whoever could rightfully claim first dibs on the historic sighting, all of them — Wetherill, Cummings, Judd, and Douglass — were on the expedition in August 1909. It is likely that none of them would have been there without their Paiute guide, Nasja Begay. In any event, word spread swiftly, and only a year later, the government declared this wondrous span a national monument and placed it under federal protection.

As Neil Judd recalled of their 5-day adventure, they set out from Oljato, "through loose, shifting sand north down the Moonlight [Wash] to the San Juan, around ragged points to the mouth of Nokai [Canyon], then up its crooked course a short distance to convenient water pockets and camping space. All day without water under a bronzing sun, across glistening sand; across acres of clicking pebbles ... across endless bare, red rocks to camp on more rocks, more sand."

They were on saddle and pack horses, and Judd's trusty steed, Brownie, grew "weary and utterly disgusted with our adventure." They continued up onto a plateau where they found water pockets, then followed down Piute Canyon, and on to the wooded slopes on the north side of Navajo Mountain. Judd distinctly remembered Professor Cummings "some rods in advance, suddenly draw rein and point down canyon" at Nonnezoshe, at midday, under a blazing August sun. The sight, wrote Judd, "awes one into silence."

Our path around the north side of Navajo Mountain took us in their same footsteps. We too felt the awed silence upon the sight of Rainbow Bridge. But ours was mixed with a hesitation to accept the reality of civilization that accompanied the sight of the boat dock and the encroaching waters of Lake

Twin yuccas, left, grace
an unnamed canyon
on White Mesa.

White Mesa, below, rises on the Kaibito Plateau in the sand-tracked hills south of Navajo Mountain.

Tendriled leaves of the yucca, right, display nature's symmetry.

Powell. We caught whiffs of the perfume of the sightseers who had just arrived by boat and who strolled up from the dock a hundred yards or so, snapped quick pictures of the famous natural bridge, and turned to go.

As we boarded the boat, our eyes remained riveted on snow-capped Navajo Mountain framed perfectly by the glorious curve of Rainbow Bridge. We left with the special knowledge of the privilege we had just shared, living within these glowing walls for a time, walls tapestried with threads of desert varnish, walls that can change a person's life. Essence-of-canyon-country days. Days amid swirling sandstone. Turquoise sky. Lizards. Green trees. Song of canyon wren. Hot sun. Rippling water. Rustlings. Whispers. Memories. ∾

Chuska and Lukachukai Mountains

Chuska
and Lukachukai Mountains

*In the Heart
of Navajoland*

Perched on the crest of a sand dune, I turn my back to the wind as it hurls blistering grains against my skin. A veil of virga sweeps over the top of Mexican Cry Mesa. Raindrops begin reaching the ground, dimpling the dune's surface. Just as I'm about to seek shelter beneath a lone juniper, a rainbow arcs across the sky. Then, a fainter bow appears above it. Each band of the color spectrum holds its identity clear and distinct — red, orange, yellow, green, blue, indigo, violet and garnet, emerald, amethyst, opal.

I recall the Navajo creation story of Changing Woman and her twin sons, Monster Slayer and Born for Water, whose job was to rid the land of alien monsters and giants. Monster Slayer used rainbows to fasten protective blankets of clouds and fog over his mother's house until a violent storm passed and she was assured the intruders were gone.

The rain skirts by, and I stay until the sun eases down to the horizon. Beams of light stream from behind the clouds and paint gold over the swirling sandstone spires called Los Gigantes. I begin to understand why the Navajo call this the Glittering World. This is their land, and they speak often of walking in beauty — their word both for beauty and harmony is *hózhó*. It is a complex

The earth has been twisted and torn on the east flank of the Lukachukai Mountains. Rock Ridge, preceding pages, is a fold, throwing hogbacks of sandstone into the air north of Sanostee. Shiprock, left, is the throat of an extinct volcano, with stony ribs radiating out onto the surrounding plains.

Sand is a constant of life in Navajoland. Drifts of sand engulf an abandoned hogan, below, along Hasbidito Creek.

Sand dunes, right, twist with the wind below Mexican Cry Mesa.

idea, central to their worldview. One should strive to walk in beauty, and if one strays, he must seek healing ceremonies to restore harmony. A rainbow is the path to follow, and a break in one seriously impedes that journey.

The field of sand dunes where I sat rests on the north flank of the Lukachukai Mountains.

One morning, Michael and I met a local Navajo man, sitting in the shade of a big, round water tank, holding a long stick with which he coaxed his flock of sheep. To the steady cadence of the windmill, he told us about bears that live up in the mountains, the livestock they kill, of how he trucks his sheep up to the high pastures in summer.

"It's hard work," he said.

Beside the water trough, a newborn lamb bawled irresistibly while we talked. The man's biggest concern was young partiers who come and open the water spigot at the tank, letting the precious fluid run out all night onto the ground. A greater travesty could hardly be imagined, because that water sustains the man's wealth — his sheep. Mutton is a staple of his diet, and

Plants seek — but don't always find — a foothold on the dry land west of the Lukachukai Mountains. The ghost of a juniper tree, below, leans into soft sand on Hasbidito Creek.

the money he earns from selling the wool will buy him gas, coffee, and flour at the trading post 10 miles down a bumpy dirt road.

The Lukachukais are the northern extension of the larger main mountain range, the Chuskas, which ride the border of northeastern Arizona and northwestern New Mexico. Their dark, brooding mass stretches for nearly a hundred miles south to Window Rock, capital of the Navajo Nation. In Navajo, Chuska, or "White Spruce," refers to the dark evergreen trees that cloak the range's summit, trees considered sacred because they attract rain. The high country of the Chuskas, from 7,500 to nearly 10,000 feet elevation, is dotted with inviting lakes and meadows of aspen, willow, and wild iris. The name Lukachukai, "Reeds Extend White," applies both to the mountains and to the small community tucked at their feet on the west side. At Lukachukai and

Small shrubs cling to eroding slopes of Chinle shale near Round Rock Mesa, left.

other small Navajo communities, trading posts, chapter houses, missions, and day schools form centers of human congregation.

Roads, mostly dirt, lead up into the Chuskas. There the view to the north stretches across the infinite Four Corners country, punctuated by Sleeping Ute and the La Plata Mountains in western Colorado and riven by the San Juan River. The east face of the Chuskas drops precipitously into the San Juan's sun-seared basin in New Mexico, out of which the imposing volcanic plug of Shiprock pierces the sky. To the south bounds Beautiful Valley, a mesmerizing swath of colorful badlands, to the small town of Ganado, Arizona, where Hubbell Trading Post reposes under graceful cottonwood trees beside Pueblo Colorado Wash. To the west, Canyon de Chelly and its major tributary, Canyon del Muerto, are sequestered in the wooded dome of the Defiance Plateau. The artifacts of industry — oil rigs, sawmills, uranium and coal mines — exist alongside old mud hogans and fields of bushy corn.

For the *Diné*, as the Navajo call themselves, this land holds sacred places, sacred plants, stories of their origins, and their gods. Monster Slayer journeyed here, readying the earth for the five-fingered humans. The real rivers and mountains of this country mark his travels and define a sacred geography to the Navajo.

The entire Chuska range, taking in the Lukachukais and even the neighboring Carrizo Mountains to the north, is Yo'di Dzil, "Goods of Value Mountain." The mountain forms the figure of a male body, with Chuska Peak the head and Beautiful Mountain in the Lukachukais and the Carrizos the lower extremities. Shiprock, floating mysteriously out in the sere valley, is said to be the body's medicine pouch or bow.

One of the most valuable goods these mountains produce is water. Tsaile, Wheatfields, Whiskey, and Coyote creeks drain the western slope of the Chuskas, accounting for most of the permanent surface water in this country. But even with these, dryness is no stranger to this land. In the drought-stricken summer of the year 2000, forest fires scorched thousands of acres in this region. Up in the fire lookout tower on Black Pinnacle in the Chuskas, the radio crackled with hourly reports from six neighboring towers — the lookouts reciting wind speed, temperature, and any sightings of "smokes." The view from the Black Pinnacle tower affords a fine fix on the landscape, and the young men who staff it obligingly pointed out significant landmarks: to the east, the bulk of Tsaile Butte and Mathews Peak; down south, the twin

Grazing has always been important to the Navajo. Cattle and sheep find rich summer pastures, left, high in the Chuska Mountains.

187

Day breaks in the
Chuska Mountains,
below.

mesas called Sonsela Buttes; to the north, the town of Tsaile; and to the west, the pine-cloaked Defiance Plateau.

The original homeland of the Navajo, *Dinétah*, lies just east of the Chuskas in the upper San Juan River basin. From the heart of Old Navajoland, the people moved westward into the Chuska Valley and the Chuska Mountains, then farther west into the deep fastness of Canyon de Chelly, where they were solidly settled by the mid-1700s.

Navajo history began to be shaped by other people's stories. Through the early 1800s, the Navajo warred with Spaniards and Mexicans over slaves, livestock, and land. The *Diné* sought refuge in Canyon de Chelly, eluding the European intruders by holing up in caves and rock shelters. A famous panel called the Spanish Expedition Mural, painted on the walls of Canyon del Muerto, purportedly records the first Spaniards seen in Navajo country. It shows a group of horsemen, one dressed in black cassock and white cross, and all armed with rifles.

A spruce-fir forest,
right, blankets
Narbona Pass.

Much of the Navajo
Nation is a harsh land,
but it is all clothed in
soft color. Aspens float
into fall beneath
Boundary Butte, below.

In 1846, the Navajo faced another new presence in their land — the Americans. Soon after their arrival, tragedy struck in the Chuska Mountains. In
August 1849, Army Col. John Washington set out with troops on an expedition to quell the Navajo. While peace negotiations were underway with
Navajo headman Narbona, an altercation occurred over a stolen horse. As
the Navajo fled, Narbona, then in his 80s, was shot and killed along with others. The battle was in the vicinity of a place long known as Washington Pass,
at the summit of the present paved road that crosses the south end of the
Chuskas.

In the late 1980s, Navajo history students at Diné College in Tsaile

Slopes of Chinle shale,
left, erode into
Lukachukai Wash near
Turquoise Mesa.

The Carrizo Mountains
form a distant
backdrop for this
stalwart juniper near
Alcove Canyon, below.

The Carrizo Mountains
form a distant
backdrop for this
stalwart juniper near
Alcove Canyon, below.

Autumnal aspen light
up the Lukachukais,
right.

wondered why this pass was named for a soldier who ordered his troops to fire on Narbona and his men. The students persuaded the U.S. Board of Geographic Names to change the name from Washington Pass to Narbona Pass.

After Narbona's death, relations between the Americans and the Navajo continued to deteriorate. In 1852, Col. Edwin Vose Sumner oversaw construction of a log and adobe fort at a wooded and watered spot on the west side of the Chuskas, where Navajo medicine men had gathered herbs and made shrines at springs. This compound, named Fort Defiance, was Arizona's first American military fort. As soon as it was garrisoned, it became "ground zero" for a series of battles known as the Navajo Wars that lasted until 1863.

Finally, in that year, Gen. James Carleton ordered all Navajo to surrender or be shot. Scout Kit Carson carried out his superior's orders. During the bitterly cold January of 1864, Carson and his troops swept through Canyon de Chelly, burning orchards and hogans and starving out the Navajo until their surrender was assured. At first in small groups, then eventually reaching almost 8,000 in number, the hostages were marched nearly 400 miles east

192

The Chuska and Lukachukai mountains challenge the common image of Navajoland as dry, sandy, windswept. While natural lakes are rare in Arizona, they are scattered throughout the high country of the Chuskas, below.

to Fort Sumner on the Pecos River in New Mexico. During the journey and at the fort, many Navajo died. The entire ordeal became known as the Long Walk. Those who lived did so under debilitating conditions. Clothing, shelter, and water were insufficient to support the numbers of people held at the fort. Navajo began to escape, and finally, even General Carleton had to admit the failure of his plan to transform the Navajo into peaceful farmers.

In 1868, a treaty was signed between the Navajo and the U.S. government. Among the first to affix his sign was Navajo leader Barboncito, who vowed:

"I will take all the Navajos to Canyon de Chelly, leave my own family there — taking the rest and scattering them between San Mateo mountain [Mount Taylor] and San Juan River. I said yesterday this was the heart of the Navajo country. In this place is a mountain called the Sierra Chusque or mountain of agriculture from which when it rains the water flows in abundance

Ponderosa pine trees swim in a sea of aspen near Boundary Butte, left.

195

Arid conditions govern
Redrock Valley beneath
the Lukachukais, below.

creating large sand bars on which the Navajoes plant their corn; it is fine country for stock or agriculture."

The Chuska Mountains occupied the center of the reservation outlined in the treaty. Upon their return from Fort Sumner, Navajo gathered at Fort Defiance and were issued rations of food, tools, and sheep. There Barboncito advised them:

"Now you are beginning again. Take care of the sheep that have been given you as you care for your own children. Never kill them for food. If you are hungry, go out after the wild animals and the wild plants. Or go without food, for you have done that before. These few sheep must grow into flocks so that we, the People, can be as we once were."

The Navajo rapidly built up their herds. With the need for new grazing lands, the reservation soon outgrew its initial bounds and was enlarged. The institution of the trading post came to the reservation, and it became the focus of commerce and contact between the Navajo and the outside Anglo world. At the posts, Navajo exchanged wool and rugs for groceries, obtained medical advice, and caught up on the news.

Two Grey Hills, on the east side of the Chuskas, is one of the oldest trading posts still in existence. Brothers Frank and Henry Noel started it in 1897. A red-haired Englishman named Ed Davies came to the Southwest in the early 1900s seeking a cure for his tuberculosis. He and his wife, Pearl, acquired Two Grey Hills, ran the post for years, and raised their family there. In the year 2000, their daughter Dee Dee returned to help the present owner, Les Wilson, celebrate the post's 103rd year of operation. She is proud that her father encouraged the fine weaving for which Two Grey Hills is known, a tradition that Les Wilson carries on. In a small room in the back of the building rise stacks of rugs of all sizes, woven in the traditional Two Grey Hills pattern in natural colors of grey, brown, and black.

I feel Ruth Begay's eyes watching me closely to see if this *bilagáana* — this white lady — can make a proper piece of fry bread. Aware of her scrutiny, I feel pressed to perform. I slip the flattened round of soft dough into a silver bowl of sizzling-hot lard. The bowl sits precariously over an open fire; a wrong move would have dire consequences. With a long forked-tip stick, I punch out any air holes that bubble up in the dough and wait until it reaches a pleasing golden color before carefully turning it. Ruth and another Navajo

Sand dunes ripple at
the foot of Mexican Cry
Mesa, right. Sandstone,
following pages, forms
alcoves along the trail
to White House Ruin in
Canyon de Chelly. The
canyon was a
stronghold for the
Navajo and remains a
special place for them.

Erosion has isolated
sandstone buttes like
Los Gigantes, below,
landmarks at the foot
of the Lukachukai
Mountains.

woman chide me if I don't turn it at just the right moment. If I do it well,
they let me know, too. When the circle of bread is done to crisp perfection, I
lift it out and gently place it in a foil pan.

Meanwhile, Navajo are lining up, waiting patiently but hungrily for the
free lunch of mutton stew, fry bread, and watermelon. I keep the process
going, turning out one piece of bread after another, then carrying batches
over to the buffet. But the line keeps getting longer. Fry bread for a hundred.
I didn't know what I was getting into when I volunteered to help the cooks.

I had met Ruth Begay earlier that morning, under a shade house covered
with oak branches. She was spinning wool into yarn on an old-fashioned
spinning wheel, praising the speed of this method over the traditional hand
spindle Navajo weavers use. She also extolled the virtues the old-style churro
sheep as she passed around skeins of the soft, raw wool to Navajo women
crowded around her.

Her demonstration, and the lunch, were part of an annual get-together
called Sheep Is Life. It's a day dedicated to the topic of sheep — *dibé* in Navajo.
That June it was held on the grounds of Diné College in Tsaile, as fleecy white
clouds gathered over the Chuskas just like flocks of sheep. Seated in folding

Sand dunes, left,
northeast of Round
Rock constantly form
and reform.

201

Thistles, used medicinally by Indians, grow near Bowl Creek, below.

Grasses thrive near Asaayi Lake, right.

chairs inside a tent, people listened while a veterinarian discoursed on sheep anatomy and diseases, first in English, then translated into Navajo. While she talked, two men quietly butchered a sheep on a table. Although most Navajo have been involved with these animals all their lives, they remained utterly attentive, eager to learn anything new about sheep, wool, and weaving.

Sheep, land, water. These important elements are central to the traditional Navajo way, ensuring that a person will walk in beauty along the path of a rainbow. For me, one end of that rainbow will always rest gently on the Chuska Mountains. ❧

202

Santa Catalina Mountains

Santa Catalina Mountains

Overlooking Four Cultures

From Windy Point halfway up the Santa Catalina Mountains, the giant, orange globe of the sun sinks toward the Tucson Mountains. Families pour out of the backs of Broncos, sweethearts smooch, teenagers catcall to their buddies, climbers spider up the vertical granite boulders. It's quite the scene on a late Sunday afternoon, as Tucsonans flock to savor the spectacular view and the aroma of pines in this mountain sanctuary. At dusk, the sky grades from peach to violet, and the lights of the city, 3,000 feet below, wink on like stars in a bowl lined with black velvet.

Between the Santa Catalinas and the Tucson Mountains, the Santa Cruz River once flowed north through Tucson. Looking south from the Catalinas, I think about Spaniards following this lifeline in the 1600s and 1700s into a country they called Pimería Alta, "Land of the Upper Pimas." In the words of historian Tom Sheridan, southern Arizona then was "a world perched on the periphery of a periphery."

To save native souls and defend against Apaches, Spanish priests and soldiers built missions and presidios along the Santa Cruz — Tumacácori, Tubac, and San Xavier del Bac. Notable among the priests was indefatigable

A wilderness of granite, the Santa Catalina Mountains rise abruptly above Tucson. The view from Windy Point, preceding pages, on the Catalina Highway to Mount Lemmon, reveals the intricate terrain. Pusch Ridge, left, on the west end of the mountains, looks down on city rooftops.

Jesuit Eusebio Kino, who rode back and forth on horseback across Pimería Alta establishing missions along the Santa Cruz and other rivers. It was Father Kino, looking north from near San Xavier in 1697, who named the massive blue mountains in his language — Santa Catarina — perhaps because it was St. Catherine's Day when he gained that first view. To the native Tohono O'odham, the range was Babad Do'ag," Frog Mountain."

Though Father Kino enjoyed good relations with the native people, others offended them with high-handedness. In 1751, Pima chief Luis of Saric led a revolt that destroyed the small village of Tubac, about 40 miles south of present-day Tucson. A year later, in June 1752, the Spanish established Presidio San Ignacio de Tubac. With 50 leather-jacketed *soldados* stationed there, under the command first of Capt. Juan Tómas Belderrain and later Juan Bautista de Anza, Tubac became the first permanent Spanish settlement in Arizona.

At the state historic park at Tubac, 4 centuries of complex cultural overlays show clearly — Indian, Spanish, Mexican, and Anglo. At the site of a small Pima village, the Spaniards built a fortified house for the *commandante*, presidio headquarters, a church, and a one-room adobe school. I walk the grounds, studying melting adobe walls and trying to reconstruct in my mind's eye what it was like here in the 1750s — the elegant home where serious governmental affairs were negotiated and festive holiday fiestas were held; the air seductive with the scent of corn tortillas and oiled leather; and caged birds singing in the soldiers' homes. A stairway leads underground to a fascinating archaeological display, revealing a cross-section of the footings and other parts of the old presidio/captain's home. The exhibit label says that three chicken bones can be seen in the dun-colored adobe. I squint through the Plexiglas, but I fail to detect them, a small matter compared to the larger significance of this historic place.

The years from 1752 on saw Tubac settled, abandoned, and resettled a number of times. One abandonment took place in 1776, when Spanish military authorities decided to move north and establish a new presidio at what became known as Tucson. That decision, says historian Sheridan, was based primarily on two things: the Santa Cruz River and protection of de Anza's trail to California against Apache raids. The Tucson presidio sat on the east bank of the Santa Cruz, and the Mission San Agustin del Tucson was on the west side. The mission, being restored as part of the Tucson Origins Project,

The varied topography of the Catalinas supports equally varied life zones. In the lower reaches of Pima Canyon, above, classic upland Sonoran Desert plants prosper — paloverde, saguaro, and prickly pear.

includes a granary, chapel, *convento*, cemetery, and garden. The Sonoran Tucsonans built their homes inside the thick walls of the presidio compound, turned their livestock out to pasture, and cut mesquite for fuelwood. They dug *acequias* to carry river water to their floodplain fields and found that wheat grown in winter was their best crop. A shaky peace with the Apaches allowed some measure of security for a time.

In 1848, a flood of Americans burning with gold fever washed down the Santa Cruz to the Gila on their way to California. In 1853, Tucson officially became part of the United States. Although no longer a remote outpost on a foreign frontier, the town's flavor remained distinctly Mexican a long time.

210

Prickly pear pads bristle in the Tucson Mountains, below, west of the city.

When I moved to Tucson in the early 1980s, I found that Hispanic heritage still strong and vibrant, though the Santa Cruz was no longer a river, and the city had been irrevocably transformed into a post-World War II Sunbelt metropolis. Michael and I were refugees from the north country, and during our 4 years in the desert, we were naturally drawn to the Catalinas. Except for the Friday night auctions on Speedway Boulevard, our major recreation consisted of trips up into the mountains, picking raspberries, cutting firewood, cross-country skiing, and inhaling that sweet elixir of the pines.

A student at the university, he would lug 5-pound textbooks into Sabino

Long aprons of sediment, called *bajadas*, form at the foot of desert mountains. A *bajada* on the northwestern side of the Catalinas hosts yucca and mesquite, below.

Grasses grow amidst granite in the Molino Basin, right.

Canyon on Sunday afternoons, and we'd loll beside a hidden *tinaja*. This, I think, is when I learned to cherish these mountains in the desert, with their incredible contrasts of sycamore-draped creeks, saguaro-studded hillsides, and snow-dusted peaks. One weekend in April, we backpacked through winter in the Wilderness of Rocks high in the Catalinas. As the snow started to stick, it became a Bewilderment of Rocks, and I appreciated the possibility of losing the trail. By the end of the day, I was wet and chilled, bordering on hypothermia. Our camp for the night was under tall evergreens, more reminiscent of Idaho than Arizona. The next day, we hiked down Romero Canyon to Catalina State Park and into spring. It was so warm we stopped to swim in pools and laze in the sun. We dawdled a bit longer than we should have, given that the friends we were meeting down in the park had delayed their picnic for us.

The constant presence of the Catalinas defined my life in Tucson. Every day, as I bicycled from work along Mountain Avenue, my eyes were drawn to

The cool, high country of the Catalinas has more in common with Canada than with the Sonoran Desert. At an elevation ranging from about 7,000 to 8,000 feet, hardwoods and a mix of conifers appear. Below, a stalwart spruce snag endures among the hardwoods.

them. In midday, their colors paled, and they looked like the false front of a movie set. But at sunset, pink light painted their steep rugged face, and on rare, exciting occasions in winter, snow covered them bewitchingly from bottom to top.

The Catalinas' astonishing climatic and biological variety has intrigued botanists and other scientists for a long time. At about 2,400 feet elevation, the Sonoran Desert's classic saguaro-paloverde community covers the foothills of the range. Their mid-elevations are grasslands dotted with oak and chaparral, rising into pine and finally fir at their heights. Steep canyons — Pima, Sabino, Molina, Ventana, Romero — slash the mountain flanks. Those that carry water part of the year are lined with the classic riparian quintet of sycamore, cottonwood, willow, walnut, and ash.

The highest peak in the Catalinas, Mount Lemmon rises to 9,157 feet elevation. It was named for 19th-century botanist Sara Lemmon, who spent her wedding trip with her new husband, John, botanizing in Arizona. In their explorations of the Catalinas and surrounding mountains, the couple found more than 100 new plants, and several species are named for them.

Another famous botanist, Forrest Shreve, was hired by D.T. MacDougal to work at the Carnegie Desert Laboratory on Tumamoc Hill on the west side of Tucson. Shreve arrived in 1908 on the Southern Pacific train, as many others did in those days. As Shreve's biographer Jan Bowers tells, "as soon as he climbed down from the train, he stepped right into the spray of a horse-drawn sprinkler that was laying the dust on the town's dirt street."

Many people who arrived at the depot would then climb into wagons to travel the 6 blocks to the Hotel Orndorff on South Meyer Street. One visitor described a dusty, but rather exotic, town:

"Passing were women with black rebosas, hiding deep combs ... men wore chaps, boots and sateen shirts ... the shops displayed gay serapes, saddles ... and many kinds of food. ... I believe I had been dropped by magic into some side street in Barcelona or Madrid."

In Shreve's time, men played the popular game of faro at the Legal Tender Saloon at 94 W. Congress. At the bookstore next door, that long-ago visitor recalled, a woman asked the clerk if he had a Bible.

"A Bible?" he replied. "Ma'am, I haven't one and I don't believe you'll get one in town."

Amber leaves, left, halo the bigtooth maples in Bear Wallow in the Catalinas.

215

Autumn colors reminiscent of New England draw people up from the desert into the mountains. A collection of multihued sycamore leaves, below, is synonymous with the changing season in Redfield Canyon.

The crimson tracery of a bigtooth maple, right, signals a crisp fall day in the vicinity of Bear Wallow.

With or without a Bible, Shreve lost no time exploring the natural wonders of his new home. A few weeks after his arrival, he and MacDougal went on a 10-day horseback trip into the Santa Catalinas, where MacDougal was studying the effects of elevation and climate on the plant life. The "continually shifting panorama of vegetation" unrolling before his eyes greatly impressed Shreve. He made many trips into the Catalinas during the next several years, and compiled one of the earliest plant lists for the mountain range.

Forrest Shreve went beyond listings and, in 1915, wrote a classic monograph in which he correlated climate and the plant life of the Santa Catalinas, a cutting-edge idea in those early days of the budding science known as ecology.

Shreve also noted that "Whatever may have been the original form of

216

Aravaipa Creek curls around the north end of the Galiuro Mountains, flowing west into the San Pedro River. Cottonwoods and sycamores are two of the "big five" riparian trees native to Arizona. A ghostly sycamore, below, adds sculptural interest to the landscape at Turkey Creek.

the Santa Catalinas they have been so far worked upon by erosion and weathering that they now possess almost no relatively level areas." Although he was a botanist, Shreve's observation that there is indeed almost no level ground in the Catalinas hints at their complex geology. In fact, they are rather famous among geologists for their beautiful, but perplexing granites and gneisses, easily seen along the Catalina Highway and in Sabino Canyon. This southern portion of the Catalinas is often called the "forerange," in distinction to the mountains' higher main body to the north.

Rock in the Catalinas dates to as old as 1.7 billion years, hard schist that

Lower Aravaipa Creek nourishes throngs of cottonwoods, left.

219

The Catalinas and surrounding mountains are steep enough that running water has carved exuberant canyons in them. Redfield Canyon, above, cuts through the volcanic rocks of the Galiuros.

was the root of ancient mountains that were beveled off to a plain. Sediments left behind by perhaps a dozen seas then stacked on top of this surface. Then, from 150 to about 65 million years ago, masses of granite and granite-like rock called diorite intruded as immense sills of rock. Explosive volcanic eruptions sundered the land, too. More granites were added, which metamorphosed into gneisses that were sheared and pulled like hot taffy. Thirty million to 17 million years ago, conditions changed dramatically when the Catalinas were tilted as blocks as part of the Basin and Range disturbance. While tremendous forces pulled and stretched the crust, the basins dropped down and the mountains rose up along faults. Erosion wore the mountains down, filling the Tucson basin with sediments thousands of feet deep, creating that velvet-lined bowl that twinkles with lights at dusk.

Owl clover, below, a member of the snapdragon family, comes in several hues — rose, purple, and even yellow.

While people may not have known why the mountains were here, they were eager to go to them purely for recreation, and for relief from the searing desert heat. As early as 1881, a local newspaper article stated that with adequate accommodations, the Catalinas "will be resorted to by the ladies of Tucson who seek to escape the tropical climate of our heated time. Wherever the ladies go, the gentlemen will follow."

Ladies, followed by gentlemen, did indeed go up to escape the "tropical climate" in the summer. By the time Forrest Shreve ventured into the Santa Catalinas, people were talking about summer cabins in the mountains. In 1916 and 1917, a few started to appear atop Mount Lemmon, coalescing into the community of Summerhaven, a private enclave within what had become national forest.

Inevitably, people wanted a speedier way to get into the mountains from Tucson. Gen. Frank Hitchcock, a former postmaster general, actively promoted a road up the south side of the Catalinas. In 1933, work began, with labor provided by men from the federal prison camp. They finished the Hitchcock Highway (better known now as the Catalina Highway or Mount Lemmon Road) in 1950.

Today, the drive up the road, and the impressive views along the way, is a requirement for all Tucson visitors. Summerhaven, where the road ends, offers both a haven from summer and a destination for downhill skiers in winter, to "the southernmost ski area on the North American continent."

Of late, with red-tiled roofs lapping at the feet of the Catalinas and thousands of cars roaring up the highway on weekends, the Catalinas have been labeled "An Exurban Forest."

We managed to survive our 4-year sojourn in Tucson. In the evenings, we walked down the street to the used book store where they let you take in ice cream cones while you browsed. We'd go to the south side for good Mexican food and out to the Tucson Mountains for nighttime picnics and full-moon hikes. We fixed up an old adobe house, and I grew a garden 9 months of the year. We ran outside on August afternoons when monsoon storms shook the fronds of the palm trees.

In October of 1983, we watched with amazement and glee when El Niño floods cut off the city on three sides. The Rillito, the usually dry riverbed on the north side of town, was running bank to bank. Michael rushed out of class on a Saturday morning, grabbed a kayaking buddy, and threw in a couple of life jackets at the last minute. I dropped them off at the bridge at Craycroft Road and drove around to First Avenue to pick them up. It had been raining nonstop for 3 days and was still pouring when they pulled into the take-out, smiling but shaking their heads in disbelief over the height of the waves and the transmission lines and condos listing toward the river.

Tucson was not destined to be our home. But we still enjoy visiting, to soak up a breathtaking desert sunset and visit the Santa Catalina Mountains that watched over us so faithfully during those years. ⨏

On the east side of
Tucson, the Rincon
Mountains share a
common geologic
heritage with their
better known
neighbors, the Santa
Catalinas. East of the
Rincons, it's wide open
ranchland, left.

Mount Trumbull and the Uinkaret Mountains

Mount Trumbull and the Uinkaret Mountains

On the Arizona Strip

On a steamy day in August, Sister Welch greeted us out on the front porch of the Jacob Hamblin home in Santa Clara, Utah, and invited us to sit on a bench inside the dark, cool living room. "Do you have plenty of time, or do you have to go soon?" she asked courteously.

We allowed that we did have time, so using a map as a visual aid she began recounting the life and travels of Jacob Hamblin, Mormon missionary and trailblazer. A volunteer tour guide for the Mormon Church, Sister Welch earnestly and sincerely told us how Hamblin came to settle in this part of southern Utah in the mid-19th century.

South of Hamblin's home in Santa Clara extends a vast territory, nearly 5 million acres of some of the emptiest, most unsettled land in the Lower 48. It's known as the Arizona Strip, the northwest corner of Arizona by virtue of political boundaries but undeniably a part of Utah geographically and ecclesiastically.

The brooding Uinkaret Mountains and their highest peak, Mount Trumbull, rise up on the southern edge of this great expanse, overlooking the

The Arizona Strip lies forgotten in the northwest corner of the state, isolated geographically by the great barrier of the Grand Canyon. High plateaus and volcanic mountains define the Strip's length and depth. Cinder cones and basalt flows, preceding pages, characterize the topography near Seven Knolls Bench, north of Mount Trumbull. Looking northeast across Wild Band Valley, left, the Vermilion Cliffs rise in the distance.

227

Views without end are
the great draw of the
Arizona Strip. Below,
backlit sagebrush and
juniper fill the valley
west of Mount
Trumbull and the
Uinkarets.

Colorado River as it writhes through the lower Grand Canyon like a brown
dragon. The mountains drop down to the sagebrush-filled Toroweap Valley
to the east, and the land swells again to more than 9,000 feet on the forested
Kaibab Plateau. Stair-stepping down to the west are the dramatic Hurricane
Cliffs, the Shivwits Plateau, Main Street Valley, and the escarpment of Grand
Wash Cliffs, which defines the western edge of the Colorado Plateau. The Virgin Mountains and the Vermilion Cliffs demarcate the Strip to the north.

A million acres of this region is now Grand Canyon-Parashant National
Monument. It's all high, wide, lonesome country. Where you can drive 200
miles and never touch pavement, where the only trace of another human is
a whirl of dust far in the distance or the forsaken muffler left in the middle

Diamond Butte, left,
draws rain from a
passing storm in upper
Hurricane Valley.

A tough, lonely life awaited settlers out on the Arizona Strip. Abandoned homesteads, below, tell a tale of Dust Bowl days.

An isolated juniper, right, emphasizes a vivid sunset in Hurricane Valley. The Grand Wash Cliffs, following pages, mark the western edge of the Colorado Plateau. Beyond stretches the Great Basin.

of the road. Where the population of rattlesnakes, jackrabbits, golden eagles, and mountain lions outnumbers that of people.

On a visit to the Uinkarets, my thoughts turn to Jacob Hamblin and the improbable scene of him wrestling a wooden boat over this wild land to reach the Colorado River. To get to that point in his life, we return to Sister Welch as she continues his story.

Hamblin was born in Ohio in 1819. He moved with his family to Nauvoo, Illinois, where, as a young man, he converted to Mormonism. Hamblin migrated west across the Plains, eventually making his home with his father and brothers in Tooele, Utah. In 1854, he obeyed the call of church leader Brigham Young to undertake a mission to the Indians living in southern Utah. There, beside Santa Clara Creek, he constructed a small, fort-like home and drew water from the stream to irrigate crops. In a few years, though, that home was washed away in a flood in which Hamblin himself was nearly

Joshua trees at the foot
of the Virgin
Mountains, above,
represent the Great
Basin country.

swept downstream. Jacob then took to "high ground," explained Sister Welch, building the stout two-story rock house where we now sat.

Hamblin apparently didn't spend much time at this new home. He was gone almost constantly, crisscrossing the Arizona Strip. At the time he had two wives, each of whom had her own bedroom on opposite sides of the main room of the house. In Jacob's absence, according to Sister Welch, the two women became close friends and were a great comfort to each other. Eventually, Hamblin had four wives, who bore 24 children.

For almost 20 years, from 1858 through the late 1870s, Hamblin shuttled back and forth on horseback, and with wagon and pack animals, aided by Paiute Indian guides. The Hopi villages in northern Arizona were a frequent destination. To get there, he had to skirt one big obstacle — Grand Canyon. For almost 300 miles, there was no place to traverse this barrier and get across the Colorado River. Upstream, the usual way was the so-called Ute Ford, or Crossing of the Fathers, where Spanish priests Francisco Domínguez and Silvestre Velez de Escalante passed in 1776 (it's now under the waters of

Lake Powell). Thirty-five miles downstream, where the Paria River empties into the Colorado, there was another possible ford, but through most of the year the river was too deep and too swift to negotiate on foot or horseback.

Hamblin realized that he could save several days' travel by crossing at the mouth of the Paria in a boat. In an effort commanding huge doses of faith and imagination, a skiff was loaded on a wagon that was wrangled up and over the Kaibab Plateau until it became mired in sand. But the party continued on to the crossing, where they fashioned a makeshift craft of "floatwood fastened together by withes." This tenuous raft got the people across, but not their animals or supplies.

In 1864, a determined Hamblin stood again at the riverbank.

With materials brought for the purpose, he wrote, "we constructed a small boat, in which we conveyed our luggage across."

This was typical understatement, for this event heralded the first authentic crossing of the Colorado at that location. It would soon become known as Lees Ferry, named for Hamblin's fellow church member John D. Lee. Soon, Lee (or his wife Emma and sons) operated a proper ferry at the famous spot. For nearly half a century, Lees Ferry served as a vital link for Mormon colonists bound for northern and eastern Arizona.

Hamblin learned all the dialects of the Indian tribes he encountered. And, vowed Sister Welch, the only "ammunition" he ever carried in his leather saddlebag was a well-worn copy of the Book of Mormon. The Indians trusted him and could always identify him, she noted, by the red bandanna he wore around his neck. Relations with the Indians broke down in the mid-1860s with the Black Hawk Wars. That slowed Mormon movement into Arizona for a time, but with the end of warfare, Mormons renewed their exploration and settlement in the early 1870s.

Enter famed Maj. John Wesley Powell, who had successfully completed an epic journey down the Colorado River through Grand Canyon in 1869. On that trip, three of the men — Bill Dunn and brothers Oramel and Seneca Howland — left the trip just before it ended. Walking out of the Canyon, they disappeared, supposedly killed by Indians.

The following year, Powell returned to launch another survey — again by river and also by land — of the immense, uncharted territory north of Grand Canyon. Seeking to learn the truth about his men's fate, and knowing Hamblin's reputation as peacemaker, explorer, and scout, Major Powell

A determined piñon
pine tree, below, finds
purchase in the Kaibab
limestone at Crazy Jug
Point.

immediately employed him as guide for the surveyors and as head nego-
tiator with the native residents.

In September 1870, Powell and Hamblin met with the Uinkaret and Shivwits Paiutes to discuss matters. The major left a vivid description of that
evening council at Mount Trumbull:

"A blazing fire is built, and around this we sit — the Indians living here,
the Shi-vwits[sic], Jacob Hamblin, and myself. This man, Hamblin, speaks
their language well, and has a great influence over all the Indians in the
region round about. He is a silent, reserved man, and when he speaks, it is
in a slow, quiet way, that inspires awe."

Aztec sandstone colors
Cottonwood Wash, left.

239

It's a long way to Toroweap, but the view makes the trek worth it. The floor of Grand Canyon lies beneath a shocking 3,000-foot precipice, below.

Beargrass clings precariously to the edge at Toroweap Point, right.

The Indians admitted to killing Powell's men, mistaking them for miners who had killed an Indian woman. But they assured the major that he and his men would henceforth travel in safety.

Powell, incidentally, bestowed the name Uinkaret on the entire range — a Paiute word which means "pine mountain" or "where the pines grow." He honored politicians and his wife in the names of individual peaks: Mount Trumbull for Sen. Lyman Trumbull, who had supported Powell when he sought government funds for his first expedition; Mount Logan for Sen. John Logan; and finally Mount Emma, for his wife who had journeyed everywhere with her husband except on the trip down the Colorado.

Powell accomplished his 1871 voyage down the Colorado River in two parts. In between those expeditions, the surveyors laid out a base line and surveyed and mapped the Arizona Strip country. In late March, they climbed Mount Trumbull. One of them, young Frederick Dellenbaugh, reported the ascent "very gradual and easy and taking the horses to the top, which was . . . 8650 [feet] above sea level, commanding a magnificent view in every direction, as far to the south-east at Mount San Francisco."

240

Powell's men surveyed as far north as the White Cliffs in Utah and as far east as the Paria River. Along the way they set up triangulation stations, often consisting of tall piles of logs and stones. One, called Brow Monument, was relocated by foresters southwest of Jacob Lake on the "brow" or edge of the Kaibab Plateau.

The surveyors, Jacob Hamblin, and almost everyone who passed through the Strip country knew well that a fresh spring flowed out of the rock at the base of the Vermilion Cliffs. It was Pipe Spring, which legend holds was named by Hamblin. In 1870, Powell attended the laying out of a fort there, designed to protect the Mormon Church's cattle herd and grazing lands from raiding Indians. This impregnable sandstone structure, known as Winsor Castle, served as residence and meeting place for settlers and travelers for many years. When the Powell surveyors arrived, Anson Winsor invited them to bunk in a nearby one-room cabin with a large fireplace. The fort and the "West Cabin" are now preserved and open to the public at Pipe Spring National Monument, where a person still can get a welcome drink of cool water out in the empty, lonesome Strip.

Though distances were great and communication slow, the Arizona Strip was a surprisingly small world in those days. Ponderosa pine logs from Mount Trumbull were sawed into lumber in mills located at the foot of the mountain. In an arduous 2-day trip, the wood was freighted over the "Temple Trail" to St. George and used to build the Mormon temple. By the time the temple was complete, a million board feet had come from the mountain. Trees from Mount Trumbull also went into Winsor Castle at Pipe Spring. In turn, supplies of butter, cheese, and beef were sent from Pipe Spring to St. George to feed the people working on the temple. After the temple was dedicated in 1877, Mormon newlyweds made the long trip to St. George in the autumn to have their marriages properly consecrated. Their route, involving a crossing of the Colorado at Lees Ferry and a stop at Pipe Spring, became known as the Honeymoon Trail.

The occasional miner tried to earn a living on the Strip. On the Kaibab Plateau, at a place called Ryan, copper was smelted for a time in the early 20th century. Cattlemen — including big ranchers like Mormon Tone Ivins and non-Mormon Preston Nutter — grazed sheep and cows, filed claims on the rangeland, and fixed water holes. Homesteaders formed a few small communities like Bundyville on the Shivwits Plateau. They abandoned

Shale melts into mud, left, as it washes down Cathedral Wash on its way to the Colorado River.

243

This cliff, below, plummets down to the Colorado River at Lava Falls.

attempts to dry-farm crops after the 1930s. Vandals burned down the Bundyville schoolhouse in the year 2000, but descendants of the first families came in and rebuilt it, showing once again the deep, historic consciousness that has always been their way.

Most of them followed in the footsteps of Jacob Hamblin, whose influence is felt at every turn in this country. It was during his extensive travels, Sister Welch informed us, that Hamblin contracted malaria. He died in 1886 and is buried in the cemetery at Alpine, Arizona.

Mount Trumbull looms northwest of Toroweap Point at sunrise, right.

Another man, John Riffey, always comes to mind when I'm in the neighborhood of Mount Trumbull. He made his home at the Tuweep Ranger

244

Station on the North Rim of Grand Canyon for close to 40 years. I first met John at Tuweep in 1980. At that time, the only way to reach him was by an indirect relay of messages between his radio and the park dispatcher on the South Rim of the Canyon where I was working.

It was March, a changling time of year in northern Arizona. I was trying to find out if the 60-mile dirt road into Tuweep was passable. Finally, word came that the road was good, so with photographer George Huey in his little Datsun pickup, we traveled over the Kaibab, dropped down into Fredonia, headed toward Pipe Spring, then turned south into Tuweep. As we approached the Canyon's edge, the road began to twist and turn amid boulders of the Esplanade sandstone that tops the rim there. Smooth, high,

Snake Gulch, a branch
of Kanab Creek, was
home to Indians for a
long time. Their
pictographs, below, are
reminders of their
presence and their
artistry.

volcanic cones — most notably one called Vulcan's Throne — adorn the rim. Road's end is Toroweap Point, where a cliff drops 3,000 feet straight down to the Colorado River. I was reduced to crawling on my belly to approach the precipitous brink.

The next morning, fog and a dark, threatening sky sent us back to the ranger station to meet with John and then head on out. In typical style, John hospitably welcomed us, made sure we had plenty of strong coffee, and bent our ears with stories of his days at Tuweep. He had come to work for the Park Service here in 1942, managed to bring in a grader to smooth out the washboards in the road, and built a dirt airstrip where he could land his Supercub, Pogo.

As we whiled away the morning, a neighbor woman stopped by to say hello. She was on her way back up Mount Trumbull in an old Carryall. John, noticing that it had started to snow, insisted on following her to make sure she made it up safely. He invited us along, and off we went, bumping up the road to Trumbull, to the school bus where she and her companion were living. Inside, we sat around the table talking and drinking more coffee.

Outside, the snow was falling harder and starting to stick. Eyeing George, I was itching to get back down and out those 60 miles of dirt that I guessed were quickly turning into slick mud. After a polite amount of time, we said our goodbyes to John and made it out just in time.

John Riffey died later that year. He and his wife, Meribeth, are buried side by side on a hill about a quarter-mile from the Tuweep Ranger Station, looking out toward Mount Trumbull. Engraved on John's granite tombstone is this tribute: "Good Samaritan, Gentle Friend, Teller of Tall Tales," along with a picture of his beloved Pogo, N1611A.

Cached beside the grave in a metal ammo can is a journal for friends and acquaintances to record personal stories of John. Returning to Toroweap 20 years after that first trip, I paid my respects to John Riffey. In the pages of the journal, I recorded the story of that jaunt up Mount Trumbull that snowy day. A singular adventure, a singular man, and a singular land. ☞

Early travelers on the
Arizona Strip followed
a natural route along
the base of the
Vermilion Cliffs, left,
heading for the
Colorado crossing at
Lees Ferry.

San Francisco Peaks

San Francisco Peaks

A Powerful Presence

A visit to the San Francisco Peaks on a clear autumn day is a treasured annual rite. In late September, from my home in Flagstaff, I gaze toward the mountains to see if the aspens are turning. For a closer look, I head out on a forest road that circles the north side of the Peaks.

To reach the glittering groves, I start my morning stroll on the Bear Jaw Trail. At the trailhead, I pick up a downed aspen branch, break off the ends, and fashion a fine, light walking stick to keep me company. The forest stretches soft and silent, the trail carpeted with dusky needles from the fir and spruce.

As I gain elevation, I come upon aspens, starting to change from summer's green to fall's fiery yellow, orange, and bronze. The leaves quake and chatter on their stems. Bracken ferns, crisped by nighttime frosts, fringe the trees' alabaster trunks.

The wine-rich smell of fallen leaves evokes an aching nostalgia. Memories swirl up like dust on the road. The short, sweet summer of the northland is closing — I've already pulled up the dry bean stalks from the garden, put seed in the bird feeders, and helped Michael stack our winter firewood.

The San Francisco Peaks, the remains of an ancient volcano, carry Arizona to its greatest heights. The tallest peak, Humphreys, rises to more than 12,600 feet. On the preceding pages, the Peaks' aspen and fir forest shows signs of winter. Flagstaff, left, began life as a railroad town, nestled at the base of the Peaks.

251

The San Francisco Volcanic Field first spewed magma onto this country 6 million years ago. Subsequent eruptions have spread a fertile cinder mulch over the ground, below.

Although it is 70,000 years old, SP Crater, right, is among the younger volcanoes in the field. Humphreys Peak, following pages, soars to 12, 633 feet above sea level.

Black bears have been seen on this side of the Peaks. If I'm lucky enough to see one here, I wonder if I'll have the fortitude to stand my ground and challenge the bruin by making lots of noise. Or will I betray the advice of experts and turn tail and run, leading the animal to view me as juicy prey?

The view north from the trail is splendid. Through the trees I see elegant cinder cones, a handful of the 600 or so in the 1,800-square-mile volcanic field that surrounds the Peaks. In fact, the entire landscape of northern Arizona is the product of an overheated Earth letting off steam. The most recent eruption — Sunset Crater — occurred only about a thousand years ago.

I see, shimmering in the mid-distance, the muted pastels of the Painted Desert and Navajoland. Beyond stretches the rim of Grand Canyon, giving no clue of the great defile that slashes the plateau. On the farthest horizon, nearly a hundred miles away, floats the dim blue dome of Navajo Mountain.

It's another 3,000 feet up to the top of the San Francisco Peaks, the highest mountain in Arizona. That distance would have been double if I'd been hiking here a million years ago. Then, a series of volcanic eruptions began that created a monumental layer cake of lava flows and loose fragments soaring to 16,000 feet. Some 3,000 feet of that rock has already been trimmed off, but today the Peaks still reach 12,633 feet at the summit of Humphreys Peak. I'm thankful for that erosive blessing, which has shortened my trudge uphill in the ever-thinning air.

From the four directions, the Peaks present a powerful presence in northern Arizona. These cloud makers are watershed and wilderness. The Hopi, Navajo, and nearly a dozen other native groups hold them sacred. Dook'o'osliid to the Navajo, Nuvatekiaqui to the Hopi, Dzil Tso to the Apache, Tsii Bina to the Acoma, Nuvaxatuh to the San Juan Southern Paiute, Hvehasahpatch to the Havasupai, Wik'hanbaja to the Hualapai, Wimonogaw'a to the Yavapai, Sunha K'hybachu Yalanne to the Zuni. Though they give them different names, all pray to these mountains for prosperity and harmony in their lives.

Seeing the Peaks from the Hopi Mesas in 1629, Spanish friars named them for their St. Francis. Further exploration of the region waited until the mid-1850s when a few Anglo-Americans filtered through, stopping at springs that flowed off the Peaks. Mostly they were trappers and mountain men. One was Antoine Leroux, son of a French family in St. Louis. Leroux served as guide for Capt. Lorenzo Sitgreaves in 1851, Amiel Weeks Whipple in 1853, and

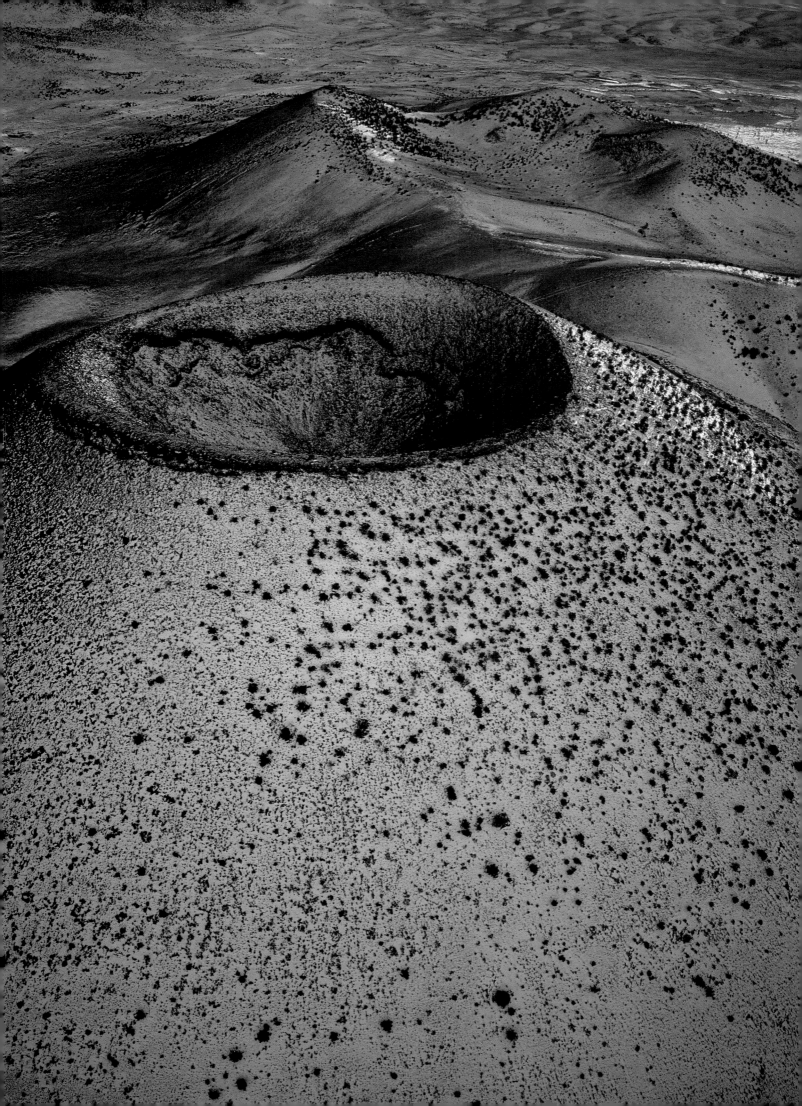

Indians took advantage of the farming opportunities that arose after the eruption of Sunset Crater a thousand years ago. They moved into lands northeast of the Peaks and built homes at Lomaki, below, and elsewhere throughout the Wupatki basin.

To the west of the Peaks, the volcano at Red Mountain, right, has been eroded into an inner sanctum.

Lt. Edward Beale in 1859 — all were federal government surveyors and explorers tracking the 35th Parallel in search of possible road and railroad routes. Perhaps Leroux was pulled by the irresistible magnetism of these mountains. Possibly influenced by the region's Indians, he might also have come to regard them as sacred.

Yet, his task was largely a practical one. Leroux showed the newcomers where to find that most precious commodity — water. Especially important was a constant spring on the west side of the Peaks.

Captain Sitgreaves, beginning to fear for the survival of his animals, welcomed the sight of that "cascading water." The Sitgreaves party camped at the spring for three days. Whipple also paused there, for 10 days in late December, where he and his men celebrated a most memorable Christmas, and it was Whipple who named the water source Leroux Spring.

Lieutenant Beale's mission was carving out an 8-foot-wide, rock-lined wagon road across northern Arizona. While near the springs in April 1859,

Aspen trees are pioneers that first return after a forest has burned. They propagate quickly by cloning and set the successional stage for the eventual regrowth of evergreen species. Grayish-white trunks, below, distinguish aspens.

Aspen stands, such as this one at Dry Lake, right, grow in elevations higher than ponderosa pine forests. Sometimes, Gambel oaks, following pages, form the understory of a conifer stand.

he found "the weather delightful; no one could pass through this country without being struck with its picturesque and beautiful scenery."

The springs (there are actually two of them — Big Leroux and Little Leroux) seep into a spacious meadow of grama grass and mountain muhly, coalescing into the headwaters of the Rio de Flag. With the benefits of grass, water, and timber, this location attracted John W. Young, son of Mormon leader Brigham Young. Around 1877, Young built a one-room cabin near Leroux Springs and claimed to have bought the land and water rights. He then raised Fort Moroni, a log stockade, about 100 feet along each side, enclosing a row of cabins. The structure, for which Fort Valley was named, housed the men cutting ponderosa pine for ties for the Atlantic & Pacific Railroad, which by that time was laying tracks across northern Arizona.

W.J. Murphy was one of those tie cutters. While he was out working in the woods, his 37-year-old wife Laura and their three children stayed in Fort

Valley. After 5 months, Laura grew weary of the wilderness: This, she said, was "a grand country in which to have a large experience, but after the novelties of seeing the beauties and grandeur of nature, I shall be done with it.... A crust in the midst of civilization would be preferable to a fortune here." (W.J. Murphy, with Laura by his side, would later go south to build the Arizona Canal, one of the first major water developments in the Salt River Valley.)

The tracks of the Atlantic & Pacific Railroad (soon to be the Atchison Topeka & Santa Fe) followed that same 35th Parallel that earlier explorers had mapped. In August 1882, the railroad had reached the foot of the San Francisco Peaks. Steam engines took on water at a place called Old Town Spring, site of a saloon and a fare-thee-well community that was soon abandoned for flatter land a half-mile back. The railroad built a depot there, and New Town was born. It would soon become downtown Flagstaff.

That thin ribbon of rail gave an immense boost to the area's logging and ranching economy. As historian Susan Olberding tells, in 1884 John Young sold Fort Moroni to the Arizona Cattle Company, and the name was changed to Fort Rickerson. Ben Bullwinkle, an ex-firefighter from Chicago, managed the fort and built a fancy barn there for his race horses. An accomplished equestrian, Bullwinkle boasted he could gallop his horse into town at 60 miles an hour!

Homesteaders staked claims in Fort Valley, among them well-known sheep men Al and Frank Beasley and a successful potato farmer, Adolph Bader. At one time, Bader shipped out 10 train carloads of spuds. The Roundtree brothers also farmed successfully, somehow surmounting the cold temperatures and the valley's 30-day, frost-free growing season. When winter winds rattled the windowpanes and snow drifted several feet deep around their doors, most people moved into town. It was tough going for the homesteaders in Fort Valley, Kendrick Park, Hart Prairie, and other locales around the Peaks. The intemperate climate, coupled with the economic crisis of the Great Depression, finally forced out nearly all of them.

During the homesteading period, the train brought brothers David and William Babbitt to Flagstaff. In 1886, they stepped off to face the town's brawling Front Street. Their three other brothers soon followed, and the family took up the enterprises of ranching and merchandising. The Babbitts became pillars of the community, helping to build Flagstaff; their grandsons and granddaughters carry on that tradition to this day.

Tourists wasted no time coming out to see this fabled country. From the

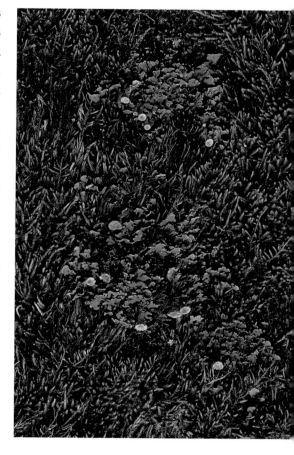

Below, moss clings to moist boulders high on the Peaks.

South of the Peaks, East Clear Creek exposes the Coconino sandstone at Kinder Crossing, left. West of the Peaks, Grand Canyon, following pages, exposes several sedimentary layers.

263

The Painted Desert, below, rolls away from the San Francisco Peaks as a multicolored land of shale and shallow washes. The various layers of the Chinle shale give this desert its name, as found north of Cameron.

The Little Colorado River, at right seen at Grand Falls, slices through the Painted Desert. Firs tower against the walls of West Fork of Oak Creek, following pages, an example of forests hiding in the bottom of canyons around the San Francisco Peaks.

Bank Hotel in Flagstaff, they could board Grand Canyon-Flagstaff Stagecoach Line and travel to the South Rim of Grand Canyon in a jostling 12-hour ride over 90 miles of rock-strewn, dusty road. Writer Charles Lummis was among the first to do so. He wrote, "There is nothing in the trip to deter ladies or young people. The drive is through the fine pine forests, with frequent and changing views of the noble San Francisco Peaks and the Painted Desert. It brings one to the very brink of this terrific gorge almost without warning."

By the 1920s and 1930s, the Peaks themselves were accessible to owners of Model Ts, who could drive up John Weatherford's toll road and be rewarded with breathtaking views into the green wonderland of the Inner Basin and the summits of Agassiz and Humphreys peaks, rimed with snow even into July.

The stunning forests of ponderosa pine drew the attention of pioneer forester Gifford Pinchot. He paid a visit in 1891, heading out from Flagstaff with mules to Grand Canyon. But the mules wandered off, leaving a disconcerted Pinchot to spend a couple days in a spring snowstorm searching for

them. Seven years later, as head of the federal government's Division of Forestry, he saw the creation of the San Francisco Mountain Forest Reserve. Local folks reacted with hostility. In the town of Williams west of Flagstaff, citizens held a mass meeting in protest and proposed sending "a man to Washington who will stay there until he heads off the scheme." Later that year, an inflammatory headline in the *Williams News* trumpeted "The Evil Deed Done," asserting that the reserve "virtually destroys Coconino County."

Pinchot returned in 1900 to survey the condition of the range in northern Arizona, then grazed heavily by hundreds of thousands of sheep. Shortly after, a system of federal grazing and logging permits was begun. In 1907, part of the San Francisco Mountain Forest Reserve became the 3.5-million-acre Coconino National Forest, which now encompasses the Peaks, the trees, the tundra, the springs, the bears, the elk, the porcupine, and all the creatures within. Now the forest hosts hunters and hikers, skiers, bicyclists, birdwatchers, and others who come to play and rejuvenate.

Northern Arizona's natural and human history fascinated scientists of all stripes. In the summer of 1889, from a base camp at Little Springs at the foot of the Peaks, biologist C. Hart Merriam investigated the diverse environments from the top of the Peaks to the bottom of Grand Canyon. The trip from alpine tundra to desert compressed in that short distance was like a journey from Alaska to Mexico. From that work, Merriam formulated the then-revolutionary ecological concept of life zones.

The dark, clear night skies lured wealthy Bostonian Percival Lowell to Flagstaff in 1894. On a hill overlooking town, he founded Lowell Observatory and set up a telescope to observe the planet Mars. In the early years of the 20th century, Philadelphian Harold Colton and his wife, Mary-Russell Ferrell, were charmed by the region's beauty and native cultures. They moved to Flagstaff and set up the Museum of Northern Arizona. From pottery and pithouses uncovered at Sunset Crater, Harold Colton went on to define a group of early people he called the Sinagua, for their land without water. From the A.D. 600s through the 1200s, this part of Arizona was a frontier: the Sinagua, Ancestral Puebloans, and people known as the Cohonina met and commingled, presenting a puzzle archaeologists are still piecing together today.

Beauty and history continue to draw people to Flagstaff. Train whistles still wail day and night, and juniper smoke sweetens the fall air. From my second-story office window in the old Babbitt Building, I look down on Heritage

Square, the beating heart of downtown Flagstaff. From the amphitheater I hear mariachi music, bluegrass, cowboy poetry, Indian drumbeats, and a little punk metal for good measure. It's hard for me to be objective about my home, a remarkable place filled with remarkable people doing remarkable things. They collect and deliver tons of clothing for orphans in Mongolia, raise money for medical care, walk visitors around the streets of downtown to look at the carefully restored stone and brick buildings. And as this little city fills in and spreads out, others campaign to save the crystalline night skies and the sacred San Francisco Peaks.

Though I didn't see a bear on my hike that day, their fresh claw marks were scrawled into the bark of several aspens. But I did revel in glorious groves of aspen in full fall splendor. Their patchwork of colors blazed against a seamless blue sky and gilded the air. Another autumn, another pilgrimage into the beautiful San Francisco Peaks that anchor my life and define my view of the world. ∾

The mountains of Arizona have been home to people throughout the past and will shelter us into the future.